Collective Memories
of a
Lost Paradise

Collective Memories
of a
Lost Paradise

Jewish Agricultural Settlements in Ukraine
During the 1920s and 1930s

Robert Belenky

Maddogerel
Publications

Collective Memories of a Lost Paradise:
Jewish Agricultural Settlements in Ukraine
during the 1920s and 1930s

Robert Belenky
Copyright© 2012 by Robert Belenky
Published 2012 by Maddogerell Publications

Maddogerell Publications
80 Lyme Road
Hanover, NH 03755

www.RobertBelenky.com

ISBN: 978-0-9851455-1-4

DEDICATION
To the Jewish people of the former Soviet Union

Table of Contents

Part I: Introduction
    The First Visit..11

Part II: Background
    Plans for the Second Visit 17

    Why This Study?...................................19

    Family History......................................21

    Russian History 24

    Jewish Dreams 25

    The American Jewish
        Joint Distribution Committee 26

    The Second Visit 27

Part III: The Project
    Day I..29

    Day II 30

    Eleven AM 31

    The First Encounter 32

    Yelena Yfimova.....................................33

    Simferopol..34

Kherson.. 36

Evening 36

Khesed Shmuel 36

Nikolaev 39

Part IV: Collective Memories

Origins 45

Invitations to a Harsh Utopia 48

Population.. 48

When We Arrived 49

Construction 51

How We Organized 51

Working the Land................................. 55

Childhood... 57

The Family... 59

School 61

Love and Marriage 63

The Job... 66

A Good Life.. 71

Immersed in Events 72

Anti-Semitism and Identity 72

Hunger 77

Cataclysm 79

"God always protects her" 86

Novopoltavka....................................... 87

POWs 96

A Slave Laborer's Story 97

Evacuation Tales 99

I Still Hear Her Voice 107

Old Friends 110

Part V: What Next?

What Next? 113

Retirement...................................... 115

Today... 118

A Yiddish Lilt.................................. 120

Part VI: Photographs

Photographs..................................... 123

Further Readings.............................. 131

Glossary of Terms 133

About the Author............................. 135

ACKNOWLEDGEMENTS

My sincerest thanks to everyone who is mentioned in the book especially Natal'ya Vysotskaya, Aleksandr Vayner, and Mikhail Goldenberg for paving the way. And to Mikhail Mitsa, senior archivist at the American Joint Distribution Committee, for his assistance and informed critique.

To David Rosenberg and Jesse Aaron Cohen, archivists at the Yivo Institute for Jewish Research in New York, for their help.

To Ruth Sylvester and Sonja Hakala, an invaluable, professional, tough but cheerful publishing team.

To Mary, colleague, critic, partner, pillar, foundation, lover, helpmate, wife, thank you for your critical reading of the initial text, your limitless support and your many helpful suggestions.

To Alice and Michael, our children, and to Sofia, Max, Ella, Oliver and Simon, our grandchildren.

Finally, to Maksim Davidovich Belenky, 1893–1977, my father (the man on the far left in the cover photo), an inspiration to all subsequent generations.

NOTE

Interviewees are referred to by given names and patronymics. Family names have not been used.

Now if you look for paradise
You'll see it there before your eyes
Stop your search and go no farther on.
There you'll find a collective farm
All run by husky Jewish arms
At Zhankoye, Dzhan, Dzhan, Dzhan.
Aunt Natasha drives the tractor,
Grandma runs the cream extractor
While we work, we all can sing our songs.
Who says Jews cannot be farmers?
Spit in his eye who would so harm us!
Say Zhankoye, Dzhan, Dzhan, Dzhan!

    — Song of the
     Jewish Settlements
     Translation used by Pete Seeger

I
Introduction

"BOBBY," DAD SAID, "I WILL BRING YOU and your mother to visit Jewish agricultural settlements in Ukraine. Someday. A promise." But he never did. World War II was responsible for the delay, and then the Cold War.

In 1997, twenty years after he died, I visited the former Soviet Union on my own for a research project about orphaned and abandoned children. One day as I strolled along St.Peterburg's Nevsky Prospekt, a man approached and introduced himself. He claimed to be a retired KGB officer. (Maybe he was.) "I knew at once that you are an American because you are wearing jeans and dirty white sneakers," he said in excellent English. We went for a drink; my treat. He consumed more vodka than I thought prudent. In the ensuing conversation, we traded stories. He said that he had spent years in a mental hospital for expressing reservations about the regime. I told him about my father's consultative work in the Soviet Union and the visit to Ukraine he had promised me. "You are fortunate that he never kept his word," the man said. "Working for Agro-Joint in those days was proof of espionage. Your father and mother would probably have been shot and with luck you would have been raised in an orphanage. Ha-ha-ha-ha!"

THE FIRST VISIT

Journal entry May 21, 2007.

Mary, my wife of half a century, and I are in the city of Simferopol, capital of Crimea formerly under the jurisdiction of the Soviet

11

Union. It is now "The Autonomous Republic of Crimea" under Ukrainian auspices. Complicated politics here. We are traveling for fun, a vacation. But I am also on a personal quest, to explore my father's role in the Jewish settlement movement of the 1920s.

My father, Max, Russian born and Jewish, had been a "tractor team leader" here in the 1920s for the American Jewish Joint Distribution Committee, "the JDC," a major philanthropic organization headquartered in New York. That was where I began my exploration two years ago. I was introduced to Mikhail Mitsa, "Misha," Senior Archivist, who suggested that I visit "Khesed Shimon," a Jewish social service center in Simferopol near to where some of the settlements had been located. "That would be an excellent place to start," he said.

Here we are. We were greeted by Natal'ya Vysotskaya, "Natasha," Community Affairs Director and manager of the Agro-Joint archives. "Agro-Joint" was the branch of the JDC that operated in the early Soviet Union. My father had been employed by JDC to work here some eighty-five years ago. Natasha showed us the archives including a group photograph that included my father. I donated a book to the khesed about the period, *On The Steppes*, by James Rosenberg, published in 1937. My father is mentioned in it.

Natasha had arranged for some very old people who had been part of the settlement movement to come to the khesed to share their memories with us. Several of them were already seated in the meeting room. "A busload more will arrive in a few minutes," she announced. When everyone had gathered, I made a rough count of some twenty people. One woman explained that she had not been a member of a settlement but was rather the wife of a former settler who was now too deteriorated to remember much.

How to begin? All of these people probably had much to say but could they be interviewed at once in one room? Daunting. Who would facilitate? I hoped it would be Natasha but she had already borrowed my camera to record the event thus by default leaving me in charge.

Our team consisted of Zhenya—a name that can refer either to a man or a woman; this one, a man, was to be our translator; Mary, who promised to record the proceedings on a digital gadget, and

Tolik, friend of and chauffeur for Zhenya. Tolik drove us to the khesed and waited for us by the car. But soon overcome with curiosity, he joined the meeting, first by cell phone check-in to Zhenya. Zhenya told him that the discussion was extremely interesting and that he should join in. He did and was visibly moved.

The discussion began with stories of current anti-Semitism in Ukraine. Swastika graffiti. Defamation by politicians. Insults.

We then asked each person if he or she would be willing to share memories of the settlements. Everybody had a story to tell, most of them warmly nostalgic. It was all digitally recorded and twice told, first in Russian then translated ably into English by Zhenya. I took photographs.

People offered rich detail; they related personal events, childhood memories some tragic, most Edenic. Throughout, the name "Agro-Joint"[1] was spoken; what it meant to them was explained: how

1. From http://en.wikipedia.org/wiki/American_Jewish_Joint_Distribution_Committee

"World War I plunged Eastern Europe into chaos and subjected Jewish communities across the region to intense poverty, famine, and inflamed anti-Semitism. The Russian Revolution and other subsequent conflicts fanned the flames further, and pleas for JDC's humanitarian intervention increased. JDC responded, always looking for opportunities to go beyond emergency food and medical relief to help establish self-sustainable Jewish life.

"One innovation was the establishment of loan 'kassas,' cooperative credit institutions that issued low interest loans to Jewish craftsmen and small business owners. From 1924 until 1938, the capital from kassa loans help revitalize villages and towns throughout Eastern Europe.

"Not in the new Soviet Union, however. The communist leadership outlawed businesses upon which Jews were largely dependent, forcing families into poverty. In 1924, the JDC had helped devise a promising program response to the situation in the Soviet Union. It was called the Agro-Joint.

"With the support of the Soviet government, JDC pushed forward with this bold initiative to settle so-called 'nonproductive' Jews as farmers on vast agricultural settlements in Ukraine, Belarus, and Crimea. A special public organisation, the Society for Settling Toiling Jews on the Land, or OZET, was established in the Soviet Union for this purpose; it functioned from 1925 to 1938. There was also a special government committee set up, called Komzet. Its function was to contribute and distribute the land for the Jewish collective farms, and to work jointly with OZET.

"By 1938, some 70,000 Jews had been resettled.

"The success of the Agro-Joint initiative would turn tragic just two years later. Joseph Stalin's government, having grown increasingly hostile to foreign organizations, arrested and subsequently executed 17 Agro-Joint staff members. By 1941, all the settlers who had not already fled were killed by the Nazis."

it brought them food when they were starving, built houses and schools, provided tractors and taught people to work the land. I was struck by one woman's story of the first arrival of tractors with laughing children riding them or running after them.

"It may have been my father who brought you those tractors!" I exclaimed.

Beautiful Jewish settlements. Enormously productive, happy, proud lives. Poor, oppressed people had achieved something of immense worth and significance.

But by the mid 1930s Stalin revealed his famously paranoid face and accused the Joint of fronting for American and German imperialists. Leaders were arrested, sent to the Gulag, starved, shot. Then the Nazis invaded and millions were murdered: parents, children, relatives, friends. Jews stripped naked, drowned in wells. Slaughter of farm animals. Hunger.

But Jews were fighters. They joined the army. They brought down airplanes. They were very brave. A grandmotherly lady told us of her life as an antiaircraft gunner. These admirable people refused to consider defeat.

"I remain a proud Communist," another woman said. "Lenin and Stalin are still my heroes." Zhenya shook his head in disbelief. "The Revolution outlawed anti-Semitism," I offered. "It dismantled the *Pale of Settlement*."[2]

Not all farm communities were strictly Jewish. A woman explained that the one she lived in was international. Ukrainians, Tatars, Russians and others belonged although the majority and the leadership was Jewish.

Relations with neighbors were good. A man told of being rescued from the Nazis by Ukrainians. Everything was possible then.

There was pride in the Jewish capacity for hard work. I told the group how yesterday Yulia, our guide at the Sinforopal Ethnographic Museum in Odessa had said, "One Jew can do the work of ten Russians."

"True, true," an old man nodded.

2. Words first appearing in italics are explained in the Appendix, Glossary section.

Oh, I cannot write it all down. There was too much. But the entire meeting was recorded. We will transcribe it when I get back home and make it into an article or a book. I will return someday, I hereby promise myself, to interview these people in proper depth.

For now it is sufficient to report that after the session, Zhenya, Tolik, Mary, and I retired to a Georgian restaurant to consider all this over a late lunch. Zhenya had never before heard of the Jewish settlement movement. Tolik opined, "Jewish people have an amazing sense of community. We Russians would never have stuck together the way Jews have in this khesed. The help they gave each other during Soviet times amazes me as does their survival during the Nazi invasion. It is terrible what they went through. Catastrophic.

"We Ukrainians have nothing like Agro-Joint where emigres help the people who suffer back home. What is it about Jewish people that makes them so strong?"

"Bookkeeping," I suggested. "Keeping track, writing, publishing. Many other people suffered, some maybe as much as Jews did. Some maybe more. But Jews record the outrages against them. We in America are aware that six million Jews were murdered during the Holocaust, but does anyone know how many Ukrainians were purposely starved to death by Stalin between 1932 and 1934? Cannibalism was documented."[3]

"Yes," Tolik said, his eyes tearing over. He went on to tell us of his family, his grandparents, and the horrors they had experienced. "So many of our people, killed. But nobody talks about us. We do not know our own story. People die in the millions and they are forgotten. Everything is forgotten. But Jews never forget."

"What is different about Jews," I said, "is that history has somehow required us to become a literate people. That is our salvation and maybe our curse. Too much thinking, too much talking, too much writing, too many holidays celebrating massacres. But that is how we remember."

"I know even less about Jews than I know about Ukrainians," Zhenya said. "I had never heard of Agro-Joint. I didn't know that there were Jews in Crimea. I never knew anything at all about Jews."

3. Snyder, "Bloodlands," pp 52,53

II
Background

Journal entry, January, 12, 2011.

I intend to visit Ukraine in April to interview people who have memories of the Jewish agricultural settlements in Ukraine during the 1920s and 1930s.

I first became aware of the subject as a child. My father made a significant contribution to this history in the decade before my birth. I often heard him talk about that period, always with animation and enthusiasm.

Recently, I learned that the settlers were for the most part not Zionists but rather non-ideologically committed poor people seeking a better life, or socialists of one sort or another. Their socialism tended to be of a humanistic sort and, before the Revolution, embodied in such entities as the Jewish Bund, the KADET and the Menshevik—rather than the Bolshevik—faction of the Russian Social Democratic Labor Party, later known as "The Communist Party of the USSR."[4] These were Russians who were also Jews, people who wanted most of all to be contributing members of the new Soviet society. Jewish identity at the time had less to do with Zionism

4. http://en.wikipedia.org/wiki/Communist_Party_of_the_USSR

than concern with the building of socialism, with having a better life and making the world a better place.

A democratic leftist even in my youth, I never found Zionism[5] attractive. It traded the humane *shtetl* dweller for Jew as Western occupier thus unfortunately sacrificing the social democratic tradition that in my understanding had been the very essence of Judaism.

From today's perspective, it is tempting to assume that the settlement movement was an outgrowth of Zionism. In fact, during the first quarter of twentieth century Russia the two movements were similar, with roots in the same phenomenon: the refusal of the dominant society to welcome its Jewish population into full citizenship. But in the 1920s, the Soviet land settlement movement was far more salient an attraction for many Jews than the longing for Palestine. This was reflected on the policy level at the JDC. It was Soviet agricultural settlement, not Zionism, that fired the imagination of Russian Jewry during the period of our present concern.[6]

What then is a Jew? An adherent of a white-bearded deity who welcomes argument? A person with a Jewish mother? A man who has undergone penile surgery? A supporter of Israeli government policy? A "cosmopolitan"? An intellectual? A socialist? A fighter for universal justice?

The Jewish settlement movement of the 1920s and 1930s contained interesting responses to these questions. While Soviet and Zionist propaganda equated Judaism with Zionism, Jewish reality was far more complex.

Oh, I shall travel. I shall see.I shall hear. Perhaps I shall even learn.

Journal entry, March 14, 2011.
I am at my desk. Alert. Back straight; jaw set; laptop on lap. Mastery of Russian language? Imperceptible. Despite motivation to the contrary, my mind wanders. My uncertain grasp of the language fizzles whether in storage or in use. Of course it does. I am a *starik*, an old guy. But what use have I for their Byzantine tongue? I make conversation quite well enough as it is. "Good day," I can say. "How

5. http://en.wikipedia.org/wiki/Zionism
6. Deckle-Chen pp 24-79

are you?" (Even, "How art thou?") "Thank you so very much." I have friends in Russia. I deal seamlessly with waiters, salesladies, officers of the law, railway conductors, little children. Unfortunately for the work I envision in Crimea and southern Ukraine—and who knows where else?—after having traveled thousands of miles and spent much money, my dumbness is bound to present serious problems. How will I manage sensitive interviews?

But surely they will provide translators, college students no doubt, and probably a few still in high school, delightful kids all, motivated to do their best first because I am a guest in their country and second because my aim is to excavate their ancestors who flourished during the Jewish agricultural settlement movement in that interlude in history between hope and despair. Yes, it might be better to speak with these people in my own voice. Yet the presence of an engaging young translator will surely contribute to the ambience, the conviviality, of the exchange.

And let us remember that I am merely an erstwhile child psychologist. No historian I

So there you have it. Buyer beware. My limitations present challenges but perhaps an advantage or two. It is too soon to worry.

Why This Study?

Mary suggested that it is for love of my father. Perhaps. Although "love" is not the word I would choose. "Identification with" better conveys the answer. I think my own career is in significant respects a continuation of my father's, at least in its more idealistic aspects.

In 1927, soon after he returned from his third and final prolonged visit to Ukraine, my father, Max, and my mother, Sophie, met and married. Then the Depression hit and the two of them faced the problem of making a living. Fortunately, Max in his travels had collected trunks full of Russian folkloric items. "Let's open a shop and sell what we've got until this thing blows over," they said to each other. Thus Max became a shopkeeper in partnership with Sophie. Very lovely it was, too, a warm and colorful gift shop in Greenwich Village, the "Russian Yarmarka," a word borrowed from German meaning "annual market." (*Russian*, please note, rather than *Jewish*.) But shopkeeping was not what Max had in mind for himself. Trade was the work of the shtetl, of his own father and grandfather. Shopkeeping would reduce him from Twentieth-Century Man, International Adventurer, Tractor Expert and Agronomist, to small merchant in the traditional mold.

Although an able shopkeeper and greatly benefitting from Sophie's artistic skills, Max remained professionally unfulfilled. He had intended to break the Ghetto mold. His older brothers, Harry and Saul, were now merchants while his younger brothers, Jacob and Allen, became doctors, all four occupations safely within tradition while Max, the middle brother, longed for liberation through agriculture, bare-chested in the sun.

As a child, I was able to relate to much of that fantasy—to the idealism, not so much to the physical labor. I had little interest in the Yarmarka except that I loved its variety, its color, its busyness. It was also a convenient place to meet my friends. We were careful to stay out of the way. The store was often my rival especially during the Christmas season when I saw my parents only in the early mornings and late at night. But my life was, otherwise, quite good. When I was little, Grandma Zhenya, "Jenny," traveled every day from her apartment on 221 East Broadway on the Lower East Side to take me to Washington Square Park. She was a plump woman, a neighborhood gossip, loved and loving. Mom considered her "infantile"—her favorite pejorative. "Oh, Ma!" she would say dismissively. You are always repeating what people tell you even when it's baloney!" True enough. But I found Grandma Jenny good fun and good company.

No one in the family was pious nor concerned with Zionism except Uncle Harry and Grandma Tamara, dad's mother, who was forever giving money to some organization to plant trees on her behalf in Palestine. Though she was a respected matriarch, her Seders were merely tolerated. My father and uncles used these occasions to act silly and make jokes. Dad was of the opinion that planting trees in Palestine was a waste of money. Harry, a somber diamond merchant, disagreed. They argued with vigorous good humor.

As age thirteen neared, I announced that I might be interested in having a Bar Mitzvah. "Why do you want to get mixed up in that superstitious nonsense?" my father asked.

Sophie, my mother, born in Boston, was oblivious to ghetto politics. A comfortable liberal and, through her Russian-born father, a second-generation atheist, her concerns included progressive education, antiques, and art. She had considerable talent in all three. Some of my grandchildren are drawn to the arts as she was. And they tend to be idealistic like Max.

Remarkable, isn't it, how shadows of ourselves and our interests pursue us through the generations, modifying in form and content with each new individual and era, alternating major and minor key yet maintaining certain themes somehow constant. In the case of our family, we all—most of us anyway—danced gingerly to Max's music of dramatic but cautious adventure.

Often an admiration for revolution might be heard in our conversation but it was modulated by a willingness to regress to a more placid way of being, and never wandered beyond reason, never became contaminated by fanaticism yet always featured progressive—if not to say "socialist"—thoughts.

Family History.

Maksim Davidovich Belenky, "Max," and his four brothers were born in Smolensk, the stunning medieval city in western Russia on the eastern border of Belarus. The family was Jewish but that city, like many at the time, was located beyond the Pale of Settlement. An exception was made in the case of the Belenkys, however, because Max's father, my grandfather David, had a trade useful to the Russians: He was a watchmaker. Therefore by the grace of Tsar Nikolai II, the family was allowed to live in Smolensk. His wife, Grandma Tamara, supplemented the modest family income by selling take-out lunches to Russian laborers.

Unlike his own brothers but along with many Jewish boys of the time, Max dreamed of working the land. Both Semites and anti-Semites characterized Jews as *"luftmenschen,"*—air people—because according to law and prevalent stereotype they did not work with their hands but rather with words. They produced sounds rather than vegetables, hogs, or railway cars. They lent money and collected the interest. They prayed. They argued. They philosophized. The stereotype fit many, but except for rare exceptions such as the Jewish agricultural colonies in Kherson in southern Ukraine established by

21

Tsar Aleksandr I, Jews were forbidden to own land. Thus work on the soil was for the most part closed to them. As for factory employment, there was precious little. Industrialization at the turn of the twentieth century was just emerging in Russia and Ukraine.

Jews were therefore reduced under law to using their minds. The few that were able to receive a formal education became lawyers and accountants, teachers and writers, merchants, moneylenders, musicians, scholars and rabbis. Seventy percent of shtetl residents were small time traders. Agriculture was limited to family plots and window boxes, the venues of victims not of those who controlled their own destinies.

Jews thus remained limited by mandate. Even under the early Soviets, it was only industrial workers, peasants and soldiers who were given the full privileges of citizenship. That included access to internal passports without which, despite the celebrated end of anti-Semitism, Jews were obliged to stay put. They could not live where they wished.

It was agriculture and industry that attracted Jewish youth of the early 20th century, work with a tangible end product, work that led to the creation of a new and better society, work consistent with the utopian socialism rampant at the time among Jews, work that dirtied the hands. Work offered liberation, a world of possibility opened first by the 1905 Revolution with slogans of equality and democracy echoing the American and French Revolutions before it, anticipating the Soviet Revolution that was to come.

Optimism, however, was sadly tempered by the spate of murderous pogroms that followed 1905. But because they lived beyond the Pale, in Smolensk, I believe that my family did not suffer violence. I have heard no stories to the contrary.

It was not surprising that Max wanted to be a farmer. There was no better way to become a liberated, twentieth-century Jew. His oldest brother, Harry ("Grisha" in Russian,"Hirsh" in Yiddish), revolutionary when young, member of KADET, took a different path. He famously tossed propaganda leaflets from the balcony of the Smolensk opera house to the orchestra below. But he grew respectable in old age, a wholesale diamond merchant, kindly and fair but hardly radical. I remember him in old age, well-dressed, at once both genial and remote. He drove a huge, black Buick with running boards and donated generously to plant trees in Palestine.

Harry emigrated to America in 1908 or 1909, the first of the family to do so. I do not know his reasons but I imagine they involved the promise that the New World held. Max and his next older brother, Saul ("Sevelye" in Yiddish), seventeen and eighteen respectively, followed in 1911. My guess is that they came for the adventure. They also planned to visit their half sister who had arrived in America sometime earlier and, with her mother, the first wife of grandpa David, settled in Iowa. I have a hazy, child's memory of my half aunt's visit to our home in New York City when I was very young.

Max and Saul arrived in the New World and hitchhiked at once to Iowa—knowing neither the route nor the English language—to see this half-aunt, whose name I have long forgotten or never knew.

Then Grandma Tamara and Grandpa David, Max's mother and father, took their two younger sons, Jack ("Yakov" in Russian; "Yakov-Yitzhok" in Yiddish) and Allen ("Alyosha" his Russian nickname; "Avrom" his name in Yiddish), and followed their three elder sons to America. They settled first on New York's Lower East Side. They then moved to Brooklyn where Grandpa opened a watch repair shop. Finally, they found a permanent home on 171st Street in the Bronx, a block from the newly constructed Grand Concourse. The area then was entirely Jewish. My grandmother lived there for forty years without learning English. Yiddish was sufficient.

Max enrolled in the Baron de Hirsch Agricultural School in Peekskill, New York. Its mission was to teach immigrant Jewish boys to become farmers. Max thrived. He later joined the staff as "Herdsman." We have a picture of him in overalls, grinning, sweat-handkerchief knotted at each of its four corners rested on his head, milking a cow by hand.

Max next enrolled in the Michigan State Agricultural College in Lansing where he studied farm machinery. He graduated a certified tractor expert, probably in 1923.

Russian History

Meanwhile, much was going on in Russia: World War, Revolution, civil war, pogroms, famine, and the building of Socialism. Jews throughout the Soviet Union, despite an attraction to the moderate vision promulgated by such groups as the Russian Social Democratic Labor Party, Menshevik branch, the KADET party and the Jewish Labor Bund, cheered the Bolsheviks and, once anti-Semitism was outlawed, joined in droves.

Times were hard. Although optimism reigned, blood flowed and Soviet Russia was faced with a host of intractable problems. Foremost among these was how to feed its people—including its huge peasant army consisting largely of people who would otherwise be farming.

Land in Ukraine was abundant. The new government confiscated the great estates with the intention of passing them on to The People who, it was ordained, would transform them into collective farms. However, with so many at war, farm labor was scarce and Ukraine, once Europe's breadbasket, found that it could not feed even itself. Besides, Ukrainian peasants were distrustful of the Soviet State and openly opposed collectivization. Famine followed famine, some for lack of personnel, some because of opposition, some a result of drought, and some engineered by the new government to "teach the peasants a lesson."[7]

In 1921, Herbert Hoover joined the effort, bringing with him the American Relief Administration composed of many non-governmental organizations including the Friends Service Committee and the American Joint Distribution Committee, "JDC," or simply "Joint," pronounced "Dzoint," in Russian. The ARA and the JDC were welcomed gratefully by Soviet Jews and with tolerance, even collaboration, by Lenin and his government. The JDC formed a subsidiary, "Agro-Joint," devoted specifically to the support of Jewish agriculture in the Soviet Union.

The Lenin administration thought it wise to solve the age-old "Jewish Problem" by accelerating the proletarianization—whether through industry or rural collectivization—of shtetl Jews. The idea was to end their role as "luftmenschen" and to create a new culture among them built on the premise that a full member of society was one who worked on something tangible.

7. http://www.ukemonde.com/lemkin/

That was fine with young Jews whose dreams coincided with the ethos of the day. An end to buying and selling. No more exploitation through money-lending or irrelevant mystical scholarship. What mattered now was growing food for the new Socialist state and all of its citizens. If others balked, Jews would lead the way.

I suspect that if Max had not emigrated earlier and had been living in the early Soviet Union, he would have been swept up by the spirit of the times, and not longed for America.

Jewish Dreams

From the shtetls in Western Russia and even the big cities beyond the Pale where few of their number had been allowed to settle came idealistic young people, a bit, I imagine, like the hippies who descended on Vermont fifty years later, similar in their spirited optimism and unpreparedness for farm life but different in that the Jews were both extremely poor and newly liberated.

They settled on land confiscated from the squires in southern Ukraine and Crimea. Much of it was in the Kherson region where Tsar Aleksandr I had placed Jews a century before.

At first these new colonies were simply small villages but they soon became the basis for collective farms, *kolkhozy*.

The Soviet government was intent on collectivizing not merely the land of former aristocrats but that of the peasants as well, including Ukrainians, Tatars and people of Polish, Hungarian and Bulgarian descent. However, resistance to collectivization within these populations was fierce. Furthermore, there was no tradition in place compatible with organizing agriculture on an industrial scale. That required knowledge, planning, bureaucracy, and collaboration. The peasants knew only how to farm, inefficiently perhaps, but their rough hands were used to getting dirty

Jews by contrast were largely an urban people with clean, soft hands, often with skills relevant to business. They were eager to become farmers but had little if any prior knowledge or experience. Unlike the locals, they found the prospect of collectivization appealing.

What they needed was equipment, money... and instruction.

Instruction? Well, there ready and able—in New York—stood Max Belenky, native Russian and Yiddish speaker, trained in modern agriculture, a tractor expert.

The American Jewish Joint Distribution Committee

Max was hired by the Joint Distribution Committee. He returned periodically to Russia and Ukraine. His job was to introduce tractors and industrial agriculture to the new Jewish farmers. He headed a tractor team under a grant from the John Deere company.

Max made three visits to Russia, each lasting the greater part of a year. The first was in 1923, the second in 1924, and the third in 1927.

Jewish kolkhozy were remarkably successful. Despite difficult times, morale was high. They survived. Often, indeed, they prospered. They became models for neighboring non-Jewish kolkhozy with which they worked in a mutually supportive manner, sharing information and resources.

The executive director of the JDC then was Dr. Joseph Rosen, native Russian speaker, world class agriculturalist and gifted negotiator. Under his leadership, relations with the Lenin government were productive. Lenin saw that JDC was able to bring funds to the Soviet Union as well as equipment and expertise. Moreover, it would solve the "Jewish Question" by offering Jewish kolkhozy as models for others to emulate thereby harnessing Jews to the goals of the Revolution.

The 1920s in the Soviet Union was a terrible decade yet an explosive, albeit often cruel hotbed of creativity. It began with famine, civil war, Jewish colonies, the "New Economic Policy," avant-garde art, the first five year plan, a second famine, and the enforced starvation of the Ukrainian peasantry.

Lenin died in 1924. By 1928, Stalin emerged as head of state bringing with him a cloud of pervasive fear. In 1937, the show trials took place, opening the "Great Terror." Stalin's paranoia was predictably aroused because the Joint Distribution Committee was both an American and a Jewish organization. "Spies!" he raved. "Traitors!

Cosmopolitans! Zionists! Imperialists!" During the 1930s, Stalin arrested and executed many of Agro-Joint's leaders.[8]

On June 22, 1941, Hitler brought Operation Barbarossa to the Soviet Union killing millions—and virtually all Jews—in its path. Some few escaped to the East. After the war many returned, some to Russia, some to Ukraine.

THE SECOND VISIT

April 8, 2011

In two days I'll be in Ukraine and I still haven't established in my mind why precisely I am going. Mortality surely has something to do with it. 2011 is the year when I cross the divide and arrive at an absurdly old age, the start of my ninth decade. The years pile on as does decrepitude in its various forms, some more tolerable than others. I am not yet decrepit but am surely about to become so. Decrepitude is a big deal. It is never gentle, though sometimes amusing.

As I slide this slippery slope, I smell senescence, the still ephemeral odor of decay. A symptom is my increasing preoccupation with such matters as heritage, legacy, and identity. I find myself writing memoirs. In my imagination I resurrect those who have gone before. My mother and father visit my dreams and I muse about Jews and Jewishness, subjects that are normally far from my concerns. The history of Jews in Europe increasingly draws my interest, particularly the Jewish agricultural settlement movement in Ukraine of the 1920s and 1930s, initiated in idealism but framed in violence.

It must be that very old people, in preparation for reunion with the deceased, experience a compulsion to know them by name and story.

There is also the matter of leaving a legacy for subsequent generations that includes taking a tally of all that has come before. The present study is a step in that direction. Through it I intend to reacquaint myself with my immediate and storied families.

---

8. Mikhail Mitsa, Senior Archivist, JDC; study in progress. Personal correspondence.

April 10, 2011

The visit draws near. I am awash in images of Simferopol, that workaday yet exotic little city, conflated in the minds of Americans with Sevastopol two hours south, headquarters of the Russian Black Sea Fleet and tourist destination.

Mary and I visited Crimea four years ago to dip our toes into the waters of the past, the culture, the settlements, the catastrophe of World War II and the Holocaust. Mass murder of civilians—Jews and non-Jews—was recorded vividly in a book I just finished, *Bloodlands*, by historian Timothy Snyder. The epicenter of the destruction began in Eastern Poland then moved to Southern Ukraine. It was there that the story of the Jewish settlement movement had previously unfolded.

It was not only Jews who perished. Ukrainians, too, having been subjected to the largest politically engineered famine in history—prior to Mao's infamous repetition of the event on an even grander scale some fifty years later.

Because much of the area was once owned by Poland, it was first the assimilated yet vulnerable ethnic Poles who perhaps suffered most under the Soviets, then it was the "Kulaks," alleged rural capitalists, who were viciously persecuted. Next it was Tatars, descendants of Genghis Khan, who were forced from their homes to resettle in the east.

The Jews, liberated from the Pale under the early Soviets, were declared full citizens by the 1936 constitution, but Stalin then murdered many during his "Great Terror" beginning with the show trials of 1937.

Indeed, under the Soviets, members of all groups were variously dispatched, shot, imprisoned, tortured, or abandoned on the dim, frozen horizons of Siberia.

Then came Hitler's armies.

Among the Jews, few survived who did not evacuate. Those that I am about to interview had found refuge in the Soviet East.

III
The Project

DAY ONE

April 10, 2011.

The lengthy flight from JFK to Kiev and the second short leg from Kiev to Simferopol were both uneventful. My major concern was that the seven hour time difference might leave me with a bad case of jet lag. I don't think it did.

Natasha, Natal'ya Vysotskaya, Education Director of Simferopol's Khesed Shimon, met me at the airport. Natasha was happy to see me again, and I was just as happy to see her. It had been four years since Mary and I last visited Ukraine. At that time we interviewed about a dozen people who had memories of Ukrainian Jewish settlements and collective farms. We learned that the kolkhozy were successful economically and generated great enthusiasm among participants. But because we were tourists and wanted to get on our way, the interviews, although fascinating, were far too brief. I was therefore eager to return and do a more thorough study. So here I am. Mary stayed home. "This is your study," she said.

Natasha set me up in an apartment in the not-quite-suburbs of this, the capital of Crimea. Yuliya Markina, my translator for a day or so who with Natasha met me at the airport, calls it a gray city. Maybe it is. But "Faceless-Post-Soviet-Highrise" is more what comes to mind.

Yuliya speaks English well, and has an engaging personality .

In the early evening, shortly after landing, Natasha, Yuliya and I hiked around the city. We drank espressos in a dark, Euro-modern cafe after which I staggered back to my room and collapsed. I woke at close to eight a.m. local time, feeling surprisingly great. But it couldn't last. My internal clock read one a.m. Despite that world-class sleep, my eyelids drooped of their own accord.

Day Two

Morning. Almost a quarter to eight. Yuliya said she would show up at eleven when we will head off together for our first interview. The goal for today is to complete at least two. I will record them on my iPod Touch, simultaneously typing Yuliya's translation into a word-processing app. In the evening, I will return to this apartment and do a rough edit of what I have.

That is to be the template for a daily, unwavering routine during the next two weeks. My plan is to spend four days in Simferopol, then four more in Kherson, a small city in southern Ukraine that had been the locus of many settlements. After Kherson? I don't know. I might just return to Simferopol, or perhaps remain in Kherson, or even possibly strike out for Odessa where I might pick the brains of Mikhail Rashkovetsky, director of the Jewish museum and a reposi-tory of immense historical knowledge. While there, I might even find a few old folks who have memories of settlements in that region as well. But leaving things open for the moment seems the most reason-able course.

Unfortunately, it appeared that Yuliya is available for only two days. She is a student in Sevastopol University and has to get back to class. Yuliya is eighteen and her field of study is Economics. "I am not sure that I really like economics that much," she confessed. "I am more into politics. I am taking economics because I want to change the world."

Admirable words. I wish she had told me what her better world might look like. She is more conservative than I am, probably because she has lived in Israel for half of her life. She is back in Crimea because her parents do not want her to be drafted into the Israeli Defense Forces, the IDF. "Good for her parents," I say.

Yuliya is a hamburger aficionado. She loves MacDonald's and could thus pass for an American teen. But she is also worldly, warm, and engaging and will surely prove a first rate asset for my research. The old folks will love her. She has the makings of everybody's granddaughter.

Yuliya tells me that her mother is Jewish but her father is not. She herself, although living near Khesed Shimon—the center of the Jewish community—seems distant from local Jewish concerns. She knows nothing of the history of the Jewish settlements that I have come to study. I wonder if that is true of most people of her generation.

"This is my very first job as a translator," Yuliya confessed. "That's okay," I said. "I'm sure you'll do very well because you love languages." She is fluent in Hebrew as well as English and intends someday to learn French, Italian and Spanish but hasn't begun on any of them yet and, she admits, perhaps never will. She learned Hebrew by living in Israel and English by going to American movies, listening carefully to the spoken words while reading the Russian subtitles.

"I have never met anyone," I confessed, "who speaks a foreign language as well as you do without having studied it. Your English is great—including a bit of an American accent—all learned, incredibly, by going to the movies."

"I have had people like you around to practice it on," she said.

"Remarkable nonetheless," I insisted.

Eleven AM

Cheerful and ready for work, Yuliya and Natasha have arrived. Eleven AM. I waited for them in front of my little walk-up apartment building. Natasha brought gifts. Russians, I noticed—Jews included—are big on gifts that might include anything from candy to souvenirs. Natasha's package contained these as well as several varieties of Crimean teas. Am I expected to reciprocate? I am not much good at this sort of thing. But I had managed to haul a few boxes of chocolates from the States along with copies of books I've written about Russian children. Books are good self-advertising but do not, I think, make proper gifts. They are not what people expect and tend to be weighty from the point of view of transport if not content.

The three of us, Yuliya, Natasha and I, hopped onto a "marchrouteka"—one of the van-like buses that provide most of the urban transportation in Russia and Ukraine—and headed beyond where we had sipped cappuccinos last night. We strolled a half mile or so further to an area that Yuliya described as "the nicest neighborhood in Simferopol." Tidy, historic houses lined the streets. Each front yard was alive with well-tended gardens; each garden contained early flourishing vegetables and patches of flowers not yet in bloom

The First Encounter

Our first interviewee, Aleksandr Zakharovich—Sasha—stood waiting for us in front of his home. A thin, white haired man, he seemed shy or perhaps simply reticent. He welcomed us courteously and led us inside where he introduced us to his wife, Maya Samuilovna, a gregarious journalist long retired. The apartment was small and old fashioned. "Just where a nineteenth-century European professor might live," I thought. Every wall was lined with books, family photographs, and memorabilia. It was a well-organized home yet well lived-in.

Sasha led us to the living room where he suggested that Yuliya and I sit with him at the antique oak table that dominated the space.

I readied my recording equipment and began the interview. Through Yuliya I explained that I wanted to hear what Sasha might recall of the Jewish settlement movement during the 1920s and 1930s. He replied that Natasha had already explained my purposes and so he began. He spoke softly but without hesitation and recalled many details. I was fascinated. I interrupted infrequently, and then only for clarification.

Excerpts from the transcript of Sasha's interview appear in Part III, the interview section, of this book

Sasha could have continued far longer than the hour and a half that we had allocated for the interview. Departure was not easy. We explained finally that we were obliged to move on to our next interviewee. As we walked toward the door, Maya brought in a tray of cookies and tea. "Eat!" she commanded smilingly. We could hardly decline. Maya Samuilovna is a warm, gracious but commanding hostess.

We chatted with Sasha and Maya for a little while longer. Finally, expressing gratitude, we regretfully departed.

The moment we were out the door, we thought of more questions to ask.

Yelena Yfimova

Our next interviewee was Yelena Yfimova, a boundlessly effusive person who brought to mind certain half-remembered relatives from my childhood, cousin Boris, for example, an achingly comic fixture of New York City's 2nd Avenue Yiddish theater world.

Yelena Yfimova remembered Mary and me from our visit almost four years earlier. She inquired after Mary.

A woman in her mid-eighties, Yelena has bright red-dyed, thinning hair. Her apartment is filled with belongings, not carefully organized as was Sasha's and not containing nearly as many books, but Yelena has far more photographs and souvenirs.

Yelena, like Sasha, had a great deal to say. She launched into her story the moment we stepped into her apartment requiring no prompting from me except for occasional encouragement to complete a story before starting a new one. She began so precipitously indeed and her story was so compelling that I had neither the presence of mind nor the time to set up my recording equipment. As a result, Yelena is the only interviewee for whom I have neither transcript nor sound file.

I shall therefore do my best to summarize: Yelena began by describing the wonderful life of children in her Jewish kolkhoz. Soon, with a segue that eluded me, she related story after terrible story of her experiences during the Nazi invasion. She shared her memories of Jews murdered both by the Nazis and the Ukrainian neighbors of the kolkhoz.

Hers was a deeply troubling history told dramatically and in excruciating detail. Toward the end, she burst into Yiddish song, "Tumbala, tumbala, tumbalalaika," she sang in her haunting, alto voice, "tumbalalaika, spiel balalaika, tumbalalaika, freilich zol zein."

I remarked on how vital she was despite the horrors she experienced. "How is it possible," I wondered, "to remain so much a part of life after so many nightmarish youthful encounters with death?"

"I have no choice," she said.

Simferopol

April 12, 2011 We are regularly turning out two interviews a day, good ones, too, but sadly my journal-keeping has lapsed. Picture-taking is now a bit irregular as well. I must get back on track. I now swear to do better on both fronts. Lots better. I also pledge that I shall remember to take a picture of tomorrow morning's interviewee and all subsequent ones.

Unfortunately, the indispensable Yuliya, my translator of the past several days, is gone. She needed to return to her studies at Sevastopol University. Yulychka (diminutive of Yuliya) is a sensitive, intelligent person, helpful not only during the interviewing but also in making sense afterward of what transpired.

I should mention that yesterday afternoon Yuliya and I interviewed a sad looking woman whose name I shall not reveal. Her transcript, however, is provided in the Interview section with no identifying mention of her affect. I refer to her sadness now only because it stood out for me. Most of our interviewees appeared anything but sad. They seemed for the most part to be remarkably vigorous, engaged, strong, often witty, people. This particular woman's session by contrast lacked a certain something. Although motivated to cooperate, she appeared quite unable to reflect, to consider the subjective within herself. I encouraged her several times to elaborate on how her experiences felt and how she processed them but she did not seem able to do either. She, unlike the others, came across as depressed. Although I had not been aware of it, I must have been prepared to see much more obvious depression in this group of survivors of war and Holocaust. To my surprise, I found very little of this revealed in our encounters. This particular woman stood out for me because she was an exception.

My new translator's name is Natasha. She likes to be called, "Nata." That is all I know about her except that she is a student at university level. Nata turned out to be brilliant, engaging, and sensible, a graduate student whiz. Her English is excellent. She will be a fine colleague and translator. Nata, Natasha, and I went for lunch together in a nearby Tatar restaurant. The food was excellent and the conversation convivial and lively.

I asked the other Natasha, my hostess, the woman who is arranging everything for me with grace and efficiency, how many more old folks might wish to be interviewed. "Only four," she said. Most of the others who remember the 1920s and 1930s are either too old and sick or have long since emigrated. Natasha has scheduled two interviewees for this afternoon, eventually another two. I told her that I plan to return here no later than the 21st of April and would do the final two on the 22nd. My plane leaves for Kiev—and ultimately New York—the following day.

Tomorrow I head to Kherson where I shall interview—with the cooperation of the local khesed—whatever senior citizens may be up for it. The khesed director there is a certain Aleksandr Vayner.

I hope also to visit what may be left of a kolkhoz. The Kherson area is where Jewish settlements were first established in 1804—some say 1807—under Tsar Aleksandr I.

I will have ten days left of this all-too-brief Ukrainian adventure once I get to Kherson and don't know how best to spend the time. Probably two or three days will be enough for that city. Beyond that, who knows? Maybe Odessa, the cultural center of Jewish Ukraine. Or Dzankoye where an MTS, Machine Tractor Station, was located. Perhaps back to Simferopol. There is always a lot to do in Simferopol given the generosity of Khesed Shimon and my mentor, the endlessly helpful Natasha.

But since I will have as much as a week to myself, I might even take a day off for sheer tourism. That would leave six days for work. Doing what? That's the question. Surely something interesting will come along. Maybe some fine family will scoop me up and invite me to hang out with them as their personal anthropologist.

What if I play detective, or rather archeologist, and dig for the shards of my own identity? I shall build castles in the sands of time in which to place and resurrect the people, events and traditions incinerated in that fearsome past. It is a rare privilege to experience history from within the minds of those who have survived it, the shtetl dwellers of my generation and a generation or so earlier where neither the angry militancy of Israeli leadership nor the furious piety of their black-hatted fundamentalists are apparent. Instead we discover shadows of aYiddish secular, working class, socialist culture.

I shall open a time capsule.

Kherson

April 14, 2011. I am standing on the platform of the Simferopol railway station prepared to board the train to Kherson. I don't know much about that city, nor how long I will be there. I am nonetheless confident of a fruitful venture because, as I have written above, Kherson is where the Jewish settlement movement began.

Much to do.

Later: It is easy to underestimate the size of this country—both countries, Russia and Ukraine. Simferopol to Kherson is a six hour journey, an aching, lurching ride on tracks in flagrant need of repair. However, it was an amusing journey, third class, punctuated by occasional, brief conversations with fellow passengers and frequent catnaps. It took a venturesome tourist mind to be at peace with teen-agers' amplified MP3 players blaring around me as well as a little boy sniveling for attention from his mother whose nose was in a romance novel.

Evening

I was met at the Kherson station by Sveta, a dithering middle aged woman who reminded me of a friend in Vermont, a bookish sort like many of us Jews in the States and, I suspect, lots who survived Russia. Sveta tells me that she is Jewish but "non-practicing." Are most Jews in this part of the old world secular? Several whom I've met appear to be. I wonder if that is true of Natasha and her colleagues in Khesed Shimon. I shall ask.

Sveta speaks no English nor any of the other European languages I suggested but we got along well. She took me to a simple Soviet-modern hotel where I had an okay dinner of Ukrainsky borscht and Cutlets Pojarsky. Cost: Eighteen dollars, not bad by our standards, wildly lavish by theirs.

I was in bad shape after a long-forgotten breakfast followed by a hike to the station, hauling baggage over shoulder and in hand. Then there was that lurching train ride described above. I neglected to mention a dear old lady who gave me three pieces of candy for no apparent reason except to engage a foreigner. It may have been my lost lamb look that evoked pity. She attempted to converse but spoke way too rapidly for my skill level. As a result, I soon retreated dumbly to my seat. A pity.

But all is well now. My hotel room is large, tidy and comfortable. The bed is firm and this place has wifi. What more can one ask?

Tomorrow morning, the Kherson khesed will provide me with a translator, a student named Olga. She will meet me at the hotel and we will go off together—"na robotaet"—to work. I hope to learn all about the Kherson khesed among many other things.

Four years ago, when Mary and I visited Ukraine, our train passed through this region, the farmland, not the city. We noted the vast, empty, black-soil, untended fields extending to the limitless rural horizon.

Now I am in Kherson City, the center of that surreal landscape.

Later: No time for interviews today. I am off to bed, bone weary.

Khesed Shmuel

April 15, 2011. The Kherson khesed, Shmuel, is a key community resource. My translator is Olga Vayner, the twenty-five-year-old daughter of Aleksandr Pavlovich Vayner, "Sasha," the center's director. Olga, a witty, cultivated young woman, is extremely helpful We work together as a first-rate team guaranteeing great interviews.

Olga showed up this morning equipped with the khesed car and driver. Off we drove to the khesed just a few blocks away. We met briefly with Sasha, her father, who graciously welcomed me and asked how I planned to proceed with the study. He appeared to be very supportive.

Sveta, the woman who met me at the train yesterday, invited me to visit the khesed library. She is the librarian. She drew my attention to a number of items in the collection related to the war and the Holocaust that, she thought, might be of use in my work.

We then met with an elderly woman, a khesed volunteer, whose entire family had been murdered by the Nazis. She told her story in exacting detail and considerable passion. I recorded and carefully typed Olga's translation of her words.

A seder rehearsal was in progress in the khesed meeting room. A crowd of perhaps a hundred were in attendance, mostly older people. Sasha Vayner gave a welcoming talk. When he noticed me listening at the doorway, he asked if I would care to say a few words to the group. Gladly! With Olga's help, I explained my study to them and the reasons for it. I invited anybody who wished to share memories of the settlements to sign up for an interview. Five people came to my assigned workroom a few minutes later. Unfortunately, we only had time to interview two of them.

In the late afternoon, Olga took me on a long stroll through the city. She has a detailed understanding of the history and architecture of the area and was a first class guide.

Kherson is far more attractive than Simferopol. We wandered past ancient buildings, a civic center, an onion-domed church, a lovely park that contained a war memorial, a synagogue supported by Americans, narrow streets where shops are now just beginning to appear. Two street musicians played beautifully. I took their picture.

As we wandered, we chatted about issues such as the quality of the modern Jewish character, the politics of Ukraine and Russia, European history and the capacity of the human soul to encompass unspeakable evil as well as heartwarming good.

We stopped at a fast-food joint for a snack and coffee. I brought up my disagreements with the Israeli government especially as promoted by such as Benjamin Netanyahu and Avigdor Lieberman. Olga seemed taken aback by my positions and I did not press my arguments while inwardly noting my unfortunate propensity to assume that everyone is in accord with my views. Besides, Israel for better or worse has nothing to do with my study.

Olga walked me back to my hotel which is even more comfortable and convenient than was my Simferopol apartment. It costs more, too. Thirty-five dollars a night as against twenty-five in Simferopol. Since I will be here for the weekend when rooms are at a premium, they will move me to a larger, even nicer one at fifty dollars per night, a whole lot in this country. In New York the cost of an equivalent room would be astronomical.

It was a productive day. We completed two full interviews and began several that were unfortunately truncated because the interviewees had prior commitments. Nonetheless, we heard much about the settlement movement and the terrible events that followed.

I find that after a short while people tend to lose focus on the settlements and talk instead about the war and Holocaust, subjects that haunt their minds. It is impossible to hold such memories in abeyance, allowing space for others. Besides, most of those we interviewed today were relatively young, too young to have retained clear images of the early settlement period. Most were born between 1925 and 1930. Their formative years were the 1930s and 1940s, not the 1920s when the settlements and the kolkhozy were flourishing.

I am off to dinner at the hotel restaurant now. Mushroom soup and pork chops.

Tomorrow morning Olga and I will interview a woman in her nineties who is a respected member of the community. What an introduction to the settlement movement! I am sure to learn much from her.

I shall go on from Kherson in a couple of days. Olga's father, Sasha Vayner, suggested that my next visit ought to be Nikolaev, some six hours to the east, a city I know nothing about. But if that's where Sasha believes I should go, that's where I shall go.

Sasha contacted the director of the Nikolaev Jewish Community Center, Mikhail Goldenberg, on my behalf.

Nikolaev

April 18, 2011. ("Nikolaev" following the Russian spelling, "Mykolayiv" in Ukrainian)

I went by bus after first calling Mikhail Goldenberg to arrange for him to meet me. Goldenberg speaks passable English but prefers Russian. I did my best to understand. The bus to Nikolaev turned out to be a mere van, modest, crowded, but not unbearable.

Misha Goldenberg, perhaps in his fifties, wears a sports coat, is visibly middle class, well educated, focused with the bearing of manager, maybe a social worker. A professor? A functionary?

Possibly even a businessman. He pulled his car to a stop in front of the bus terminal. "Bob?" he asked. "Misha!" He opened the passenger-side door for me with a greeting in comprehensible English. I thanked him in questionable Russian and tossed my bags into the trunk, entered the car and off we went.

We drove through Nikolaev. Conversation was minimal. Mild discomfort was in the air. I gazed out the window. We drove down a broad main avenue, past shops, a park, a tall church spire. Not many cars. US-style fast food restaurants. A woman walking purposefully, a man strolling, children holding their mothers' hands, teenagers barreling along gracefully on skateboards. A sign, in Russian, "Pizza and Chinese Dinners."

Nikolaev struck me as commercial, attractive, informal, alive.

Later: I walked alone through the city. A man on a bench played the accordion and sang in a gravely voice, his hat turned upside down on the sidewalk inviting donations. A few people tossed in coins, I among them.

The Jewish Community Center is a three-story brick building on a tidy street some blocks from the center of town. Suburban. Could be Brooklyn. There is a sign in Russian on the building. I can read it. "Khesed," it says plus several additional words unknown to me followed by "Jewish Community Center." Misha informs me that the center is on the second floor. The khesed is on the first.

"The khesed alone was not enough for this community," Misha explained. "The Jews of Nikolaev needed more." He continued switching casually from accented English to Russian and back. "The khesed is only for social work, for people who have problems, people who need help. That's fine, but we also must have a center that serves everyone, not just those in critical need. I have been on the board of the khesed that continues to serve an important function. But after some years I decided to create the Community Center using funds from my engineering business and with the help of others including friends in America. Did I tell you that I am an engineer?

"We have social and cultural events here, music, dances, and outings. The khesed serves many important functions. We used to be located elsewhere but I bought this building and renovated it so that now it serves both the khesed and the center. They are distinct organizations but work together seamlessly. Rebuilding the Jewish community in Nikolaev needs both but requires a big effort."

A tall, smiling woman stood at the door of an office to which Misha was leading me. "This is Olga Ivanova," he explained. "She will be your translator. She is very good."

"Pleased to meet you," I said.

"Your project sounds interesting," she said. "I hope I can help."

Olga is in her mid-thirties, a partner in her family's travel agency. She has an intelligent manner combined with an upbeat, irreverent sense of humor. I was interested to learn that she is Ukrainian, not Jewish.

"I love working for the Jewish Center," she said. "Jews know how to get things done. They are organized and committed. Jewish people appreciate each other and collaborate in a good way and what they accomplish is very helpful to their members. We have nothing like this within the Ukrainian community or the Orthodox Church, no social services at all and no activities. I help out here on a part time basis when I can find the time. I translate. I teach children. Sometimes they ask me to lead a group of one sort or another for older people."

"I think we shall work together well," I said.

Golenberg then introduced me to the former director of the Nikolaev Jewish Museum, Irina Alekseevna. "She will give you an historical overview of our area," he said.

My notes from that overview follow:

"History:

"The first Jewish agricultural settlement in the Russian Empire was in 1807 under Tsar Aleksandr I. By 1810 there were nine settlements in Ukraine. There were 6,000 families or 36,400 people altogether. They were sent to get rid of them from the cities and thus to resolve the eternal "Jewish Question." They did not leave of their own free will.

"Earlier, in 1762, Catherine the Great declared that everyone except Jews was invited to come and settle this region. Then in 1769, she added permission for Jews. Jewish settlements began in1803 although the exact year is uncertain. Kherson was founded in 1778.

By the 1780s, there were already a few Jews here. In 1799, there were thirty-nine Jewish traders and one hundred eighty Jewish citizens. By 1803, there were thirty-six businessmen and three hundred thirty-three Jewish citizens.

"By 1810 there were eight or nine colonies here. The Jewish Question had to do with problems in Poland. Aleksandr I decided that all Jews were required to become farmers, not just business people. They were compelled to join the colonies. This compulsion oddly contradicted the Russian Empire policy forbidding Jews to own land. It became the basis of irreverent humor among us, "Jewish farmers? A joke!" The meaning is that on the one hand, Jews are not allowed to own land. On the other hand, the Tsar forced us onto the land.

"At the conclusion of the Russian-Turkish war, this region was reputedly uninhabited. Ukraine was known then as "New Russia" or "Little Russia."

"Between 1836 and1850, the biggest wave of agricultural colonists were Jews. They came mostly from Belarus and Lithuania.

"The name Finkelstein was prominent among the first thirty-six families who settled in the city of Kherson. It was a hard life here for everyone but better than what they experienced in Belarus and Lithuania. As the government spread positive information about conditions here to Western Russia, more and more Jewish people showed an interest in coming. But, once here, they found nothing. The government announced that it would pay them to remain, but corrupt officials on the local level often stole the money.

"There was no water and settlers didn't know how to work the land. But there was an ethnic German settlement already here and the Germans willingly taught the Jews to farm.

"As a result of all the hardships, some of the Jewish emigrants returned to the cities but those who remained eventually became excellent farmers. After a few years, they did better than their traditional neighbors, the Germans and others. In fact, most did decide to remain and to spend their lives working the land.

"The colonies were originally very separate one from another with little cooperation among them.

"I have been describing the situation of the colonies during the

19th century. In the 20th century, however, under Argo Joint, cooperation in a Socialist, communal sense was encouraged and developed apace."

"Massacres:

"Information may be found in our khesed library about a settlement where hundreds of Jews were massacred by the Nazis and their local collaborators. Another such settlement is in the Brunsky region. A thousand people are lying there. All of these settlements, nine altogether, were connected to each other."

IV
Collective Memories

WHAT FOLLOWS ARE EXCERPTS from transcripts of the interviews that
I collected in this study. They are organized by topic. Within each
topic, stories are included from one or more of the interviewees. The
emphasis is on the subject matter rather than on the person telling
the story although a sense of the individual may be gained by following his or her interview over several topics.

I have neither elaborated nor editorialized and have edited only
minimally.

Origins

ALEKSANDR ZAKHAROVICH

We lived in the Smolensk oblast—"district" as you say in
English—in a town called Hislevichi. My father had a big family that
included parents, brothers, sisters, children, and we lived together
in a big house. My father and his brothers had a woodcraft business;
they made things from "klon" as it is called in Russian, "maple" in
English.

LYUDMILA ALEKSANDROVNA

I was born in 1928 on the 5th of December. My father had already
emigrated to America. Every week he sent money home. He went to
America because Jews were not permitted to live on the land in
Russia.

My father was a very successful mechanic. He would get over-time bonuses and even more on the weekends. This was before I was born.

My father returned in 1926 to Crimea from Gomel in Belarus where my parents lived for a while because my sister was very sick with asthma. Many Jewish people came to Crimea then for their health so he thought it would be good for her. It might help her asthma, he thought.

YFIM GREGORIEVICH

My father worked in a factory. Our mother was a housewife. We lived near here, in Kherson. This was our home.

ANNA ISRAELEVNA

I was born on July 20, 1920, in the center of Kalinindorf which is in the Kherson oblast. It was a big village, founded in 1808, two hundred and three years ago.

All my family was born there, my mother, father, grandparents; even my oldest son. We all were born there.

LISA EFIMOVNA

I was born 1916, 25 December, in the Kevogradskaya Oblast, Ustinovski Rayonne in the Jewish colony of Sagaidak. Ours was a religious family. My mother died when I was just one month old.

Just before she died, my mother asked her mother-in-law to raise me and to make sure that her husband would marry again but only that I not be raised by his new wife, my stepmother.

So I lived with my father and grandmother for seven years after which my father married for the second time but, according to my mother's wishes, I remained with my grandmother. I didn't know that she was my grandmother. I called her "mother."

LYDYA BORISOVNA

I was born 16 June, 1924, in Darnitsa in the Kiev oblast (province.) My parents were foresters. In 1930, I don't know if it was a legal requirement, but they were told to settle in Crimea. They moved to the Sakisky District of Delitz—the name of the kolkhoz. There were only two barracks there at the time and no houses. We lived in one of those these barracks.

ASYA MOYESEVOVNA

I was born on June 15, 1919. Our kolkhoz started in 1928. My mother worked there as an accountant. My father died in September, 1927, after ten years of Soviet power. There were three children in my family, me and younger twins who were born in January, 1927.

LYUDMILA ALEKSEEVNA

I was born in 1942. My father lived in the Nikolaev oblast. During the 1920s, my family had to run away from there because of the pogroms. We then lived in the village of Romonovka, in the Kherson oblast.

ANNA IOSIFOVNA (RUSSIAN)/HANNAH SHIFREH (YIDDISH)

I was born on 15 November, 1924. We had no documents with us when we came to Crimea, so there is a difference between my real name and birthdate and what is written on my internal passport.

My family was originally from Smolensk, actually it was a shtetl near Smolensk called Hislevichi. My father was in the army in World War I on the Russian side. He was a prisoner of war in Germany when peace was signed. And he had been injured. He had problems with his hand. Because of this he was given a choice by the government of where to live.

IRINA ALEKSEEVNA

I was born in the city of Kustanai, Kazakhstan, in August, 1945. There was my mother, brother, and sister, Masha, who was born in 1931. Rita, my other sister, was born in 1936. Both are still alive. My mother worked at the train station in Kazakhstan. My mother and father met in Kiev and after a few years, came to Kherson. The whole family including my paternal grandparents also settled in Kherson but my maternal grandparents lived in Kiev.

SOFIA IVANOVNA

I was born 19 January, 1920. What I remember learning from my father and my grandmother is that they were taken from the little town of Latiki in the Chernigov oblast, which is a region in Crimea. Latiki belonged to Belarus back then but now it belongs to Ukraine. Our family ended up not where we expected. It was a place close to Kurman-Kemelchi that is now called Krasnosavodsk; a community seven kilometers away called Nialeben, a kolkhoz, a Jewish agricultural settlement. The name is Yiddish. It means "New Life." The houses were built by Agro-Joint.

OLGA SIMONOVNA

I was born April 7,1928. I remember the kolkhoz where we lived but I don't remember the beginning. I was only a year and a half old then.

Invitations to a Harsh Utopia

ALEKSANDR ZAKHAROVICH

Right after the Revolution all of the businesses were closed, especially the small ones. There was no way to make a living. Fortunately, our family was invited to come to the unsettled Crimean lands. Representatives of the government organization, *Ozet*, came to our house and told us how great life would be for us in Crimea. They rounded up a lot of people and persuaded them to go. It was voluntary. Nobody was forced.

ASYA MOYESEVOVNA

Before moving to the kolkhoz, we lived in a village near Moscow called Dobry. In 1933, one of the kolkhoz men, an ethnic German, was sent to us to convince us to come to the kolkhoz. We came and I lived there for only a year—until 1934.

SOFIA IVANOVNA

Why did we come in 1929? Agro-Joint brought us. I cannot say that anybody forced us. But I do know that the Joint helped make the kolkhoz attractive for us. We did not move for economic reasons. But we were given houses here and everything we needed. Agro-Joint even gave us seeds to plant in the fields. It was a good deal.

Population

ALEKSANDR ZAKHAROVICH

The kolkhoz did not consist only of Jews. In my settlement there were two Russian families. A Bulgarian family lived near the cistern and grew vegetables there.

When the Nazis invaded, they did not destroy the kolkhozy, they simply renamed them. They referred to them as *obschinach*, communities, rather than *kolkhozy*, collective farms. But the Jewish kolkhozy did not remain exclusively Jewish under the Nazis. As Jews were massacred, people of other nationalities joined and the kolkhozy continued.

When We Arrived
ALEKSANDR ZAKHAROVICH

The men in our family came here beginning in 1929. My father was one of the first. He bought land in Crimea because it was said that the soil was very rich.

Then, after my father, the rest of us arrived in 1930. The government gave each family a wagon for moving. We put all our things in the wagon including personal items. Every family had the right to bring a half ton of potatoes.

We arrived in Kolai which before we came had only one tractor for the entire community. But Ford tractors were here by the time we arrived. The John Deeres came later.

It was only Jewish people who moved to Crimea. The Russians stayed where they were. They bought up the stuff that the Jews had to leave behind.

We had sold our house and a fur coat in Hislevichi before we moved. So we had some money to begin with. By the end of 1929, each family had earned enough through agriculture that we had the possibility of buying what we needed beyond the basics.

Our family bought a cow. We needed it for the milk because we couldn't afford meat. We had small children who required nourishing food.

Soon after we arrived, we also bought a horse we named Regina which means "Red Head" and then a couple of chickens. It was a very exciting time for us children.

In 1929 each family was given a small parcel of land. Agro-Joint dug wells for us, some of them were 112 meters deep. A diesel motor became available to bring up the water. Before that, it had been like a desert here. Finding water was necessary but extremely difficult. It required large machines and substantial digging.

Life was not easy. In the winter it got very cold. So we built a traditional ovencalled a *gruba* that we could sleep on. There was no wood to burn so we burned peat.

LYUDMILA ALEKSANDROVNA

We moved a lot. My father took our family from Crimea to Leningrad because my mother had relatives there and after that we moved back again to Gomel in Belarus. When we were in Gomel, we got a letter that in Crimea they had a very good harvest. So we went back to Crimea.

We came to an area called the 49th District. A lot of German people were there. Freidorf, "Freetown," is what their kolkhoz was called. Then it was renamed a couple of times.

Papa quickly got promoted and soon he became the head of the whole area through the local soviet. But then he got into an accident.

As he was getting out of the car, he broke his pelvis. They put him in the hospital in the 62nd District where there was a very good doctor. When he got out of the hospital, he was an invalid and couldn't do anything. The doctor suggested that he become the official who takes care of both the inventory and the people who work in the hospital. So we moved to this 62nd Settlement where he could function in that capacity.

OLGA SIMONOVNA

My father was a Komsomol leader and we lived in Genitchesk in the Kherson oblast. Agro-Joint was gathering people and getting them to emigrate to certain remote places to develop kolkhozy. My dad was an organizer for the Saki area in Crimea.

ASYA MOYESEVOVNA

Many of my relatives went to Moscow when collectivization began, but I came to Nikolaev to be with my aunt, my father's sister.

ANNA IOSIFOVNA (RUSSIAN)/HANNAH SHIFREH (YIDDISH)

We came to Crimea in 1926 when I was two or three. When we arrived, there was nothing, nothing but steppe between Kazan and Azov. My grandfather got here first in 1924. He built a house and then his oldest son, my uncle, came with his family. Two years later the rest of us followed.

SOFIA IVANOVNA

Why did we come in 1929? Agro-Joint brought us. I cannot say that anybody forced us. But I do know that the Joint helped us in many ways. We did not move for employment. We had houses here and everything we needed. Agro-Joint even gave us seeds to plant in the fields.

The Jews in Latiki were gathered together and brought to Crimea. There were a lot of places for Jews to live within a few kilometers of where we were brought. All the buildings looked alike. There were two streets, the upper one and the lower one. We had a store and big family garden plots.

We called our kolkhoz "Nialeben," Yiddish for New Life.

Construction

ALEKSANDR ZAKHAROVICH

We built our houses of "calib," a construction material that is something like concrete. It is bricks made of mud and straw. We did not put animal feces into the mix because initially we did not have enough animals. We mashed it all together and poured the result into forms. Then we baked it in the sun. When it became hard, we made houses out of it.

Crimea was empty then, a land without anything. But in just one year we built twenty to thirty houses. We did this in Dzankoye, the railway junction town where there was also the central MTS or tractor station. We built on a former aristocrat's large, confiscated estate some twenty kilometers from the Russian village of Kolai which now is called Azofskia.

All the houses we built were exactly the same. We put on the same windows, doors, and the same red roof.

How We Organized

ALEKSANDR AAKHAROVICH

By 1930 we began to organize the kolkhoz. Our settlement was called Rattendorf and consisted of 35 families. The government supplied us with a secretary. The kolkhoz was like a government organization. Two Communists were in the leadership. The head man had the backing of the Party. His name was Yefim Markovitz Weiseman.

51

Leaders were imposed on us under pressure. It was not a democracy.

At that time we put all the farm animals from all the families in one place. We selected people who were to take responsibility for the entire farm including all the animals and declared such people "Specialists." But each family knew which animals were theirs and were responsible for them. I remember that one horse was named "Mishka Rosenblum" because he belonged to the Rosenblum family. Every Jewish man decided that he was going to watch after the particular animals that he had contributed. People received payment in food. It was basically a barter system.

Life was not easy. There were many squabbles and arguments.

The inventory was contributed by Agro-Joint.

The kolkhoz consisted of two and a half thousand hectares of land. Of this, fifteen hundred was for the animals and, eventually, crops, the rest was for housing.

Initially nothing was cultivated. Nothing was growing. But soon we were planting wheat, barley, and rye. What we did not use to sow grain we kept aside as grazing land for the animals.

Then came the 1930s. In 1931 production was extremely poor. The country was in great difficulty. So were we. But we learned. Because we did not at first know how to work the land, we studied agriculture. We studied everything that we needed to know and learned quickly, as quickly as we could.

We were paid in a system of work days. Each day when we went to work, we would get credit but not just for the time spent. It was a matter of how much a person actually produced.

LYUDMILA ALEKSANDROVNA

My father suggested to all the people living in this settlement that they get together and buy a tractor from Agro-Joint. So they bought one tractor. My father was very well educated so he became head of the kolkhoz.

I began to work when I was fourteen because the workers were given 500 grams of bread but to non-workers it was just 300. I needed the job and my family needed bread.

ANNA IOSIFOVNA (RUSSIAN)/HANNAH BASILA SHIFREH (YIDDISH)

The community was arranged in sections that were small groups of houses. There was a Russian settlement in Crimea in which there were several sections. It is called the Krasnosavodsky Rayonne. That's where we lived.

We were in the fourth section. Each section was separated from the others by about three kilometers. During the years of 1928, 1929, and 1930, the sections governed themselves. Construction of houses took place within the section.

The sections had a common center where we were given rules that we followed.

Agro-Joint helped us considerably and I can't think about it even now without tears of gratitude. The Joint bought us a cow. It helped us build our house. We made wooden forms to create bricks from straw and loam and with them we constructed the houses.

We finished the houses in 1930. We all worked together in the fields. We sowed seeds together. It was wonderful.

But life was hard. We were stuck there. We had no internal passports; no documents at all so we could not travel anywhere.

But I received the proper documents when I was maybe fourteen when the kolkhoz was organized in 1931. Our family also had sa small plot of our own land that we worked for ourselves in addition to the collective. But we worked mostly for the kolkhoz and contributed what we could to it. We had two horses of our own that we gave to the kolkhoz.

ALEKSANDR ZAKHAROVICH

It was known in Crimea at the time that Jewish kolkhozy were the best. People lived very well within them for years, thirty five or thirty six years in some cases. Kolkhozy varied considerably one from another, often according to nationality. For example, Tatar kolkhozy did not have wood floors but in those of the ethnic Germans, wood was used with skilled craftsmanship for floors among other things.

LYUDMILA ALEKSANDROVNA

The main thing is that Jewish kolkhozy were very successful in our area despite the famine. A lot of people think Jews can't work on the land—that they are congenitally no good at farming—but such people are wrong. Jews in fact did everything very well. They worked the tractors. They worked the combines. My father, for example, did many jobs. He was excellent at all of them even though he was an invalid.

Then my father was asked to work at a tractor station in another town in the 62nd section. He worked there very well until the start of the war.

SOFIA IVANOVNA

Naileben was a kolkhoz and Jews lived and worked there. It was so productive that it was nominated for a prize in Moscow at some kind of fair. Naileben was called a "millionaire kolkhoz" because it was so prosperous. It was number one in all of Crimea.

LYUDMILA ALEKSANDROVNA

I had an older brother. We came here with him. My two sisters were born after we arrived here. Our family was very poor. But eventually we had a cow, chickens, and ducks. When we joined the kolkhoz, we were given labor books, not internal passports, you understand, but simply labor books. Our work efforts were recorded there. At the end of the year, we were given food according to the work we did.

We gradually became wealthier. My mother baked bread. My father worked in the kolkhoz but I don't remember exactly what he did.

We were sent tractors from the MTS in Dzankoye. It was 1935 or maybe 1936 that we got them. Anyway, it was before the war.

In 1931 and 1932, the government declared that the help of Agro-Joint was no longer needed. They believed we were already well off and we did not need further help. I was only a girl so I didn't know.

ANNA ISRAELEVNA

Before 1928, people did not work collectively. Everyone was separate, out for themselves. But with the start of the kolkhoz system, things got better, much better. We all became successful. Our kolkhoz became the first million-ruble kolkhoz in the Soviet Union.

Its name was, "The Way to Socialism." We were very proud of it because it was a Jewish kolkhoz and it was such an honor to be so wealthy.

LYDYA BORISOVNA

My mother didn't look Jewish and it was uncommon for Jews to be milkmaids. People couldn't believe that she was a Jewish milkmaid.

Working the Land

ALEKSANDR ZAKHAROVICH

By 1935, things became easier. The harvest was good. In my house, there was a window. Looking through it we could see where the kolkhoz had deposited one and a half tons of seed. Our family by then already had two cows and two calves. Life had become good.

LYUDMILA ALEKSEEVNA

We worked hard in the kolkhoz. It was a very good place. Everything was mechanized. And everyone cooperated and shared.

ANNA ISRAELEVNA

In 1925 when I was small, the first tractor came to our community. The tractor was a little Ford with wheels rather than tracks. It was an unbelievable thing for us because it moved on its own without horses. All of us kids were so very excited and inspired. My brother—he was eleven then—came back home after seeing the tractor. He said that if he ever got a job driving a tractor, he would be the happiest man in the world. And after the 7th grade he went to take tractor courses at the technical school and he did become a tractor operator. He worked on tractors even before his eighteenth birthday.

At eighteen, he had to go to the army where he became a pilot. He survived. He married and had a son and lived in Borispol near Kiev where there was a military airport.

Agro-Joint had a program for building houses. From 1918 to 1923, the Joint built twenty-two *pasoluk*, farm communities like hutors. They all were very pretty and had cows, chickens and were settled by Jews from small *mestetchka* and from the cities. My father was a builder. Jewish people—especially from the cities—wanted to live in those houses that he helped build.

When they lived in a mestetchka, people were used to working hard. They had been cleaners and traders. They collected scrap metal. They were shoemakers and tailors. They made shoes and clothing.

In the new villages, the settlements, there was more prosperity and more diversity of occupation. People had land and horses. They worked the land.

In 1928, there was a collectivization program. Everybody was poor at the time. Every poor, Jewish settler wanted to join a kolkhoz. But the rich people, the *kulaks*, didn't want to. They used the poor farmers as slaves. A rich kulak would hire poor farmers to work on his land and then when the job was done, he used the poor farmers' horses to work some more. This was exploitation. The kolkhoz was much more democratic. There was no exploitation.

[She bursts into tears]

LYDYA BORISOVNA

One day a leader of Agro-Joint came to our kolkhoz. He brought cows and tractors with him from America. I rode one of those tractors. He took the tractors through the countryside and allowed children to drive them alongside of him.

Our mother worked as a milkmaid. She did this until the war began. Papa worked in the field with tractors, combines, seeders and so on.

We constructed schools and houses. A house was usually one building with two owners; two apartments and two exits. The Joint did all this. They brought material and so on and so forth but we did the work. People started to come to this collective farm. Not only Jewish people but Russians, Ukrainians, and Tatars. It was international.

Our kolkhoz was very successfuk and we worked there until the war. We made bread and milk. We produced seeds. Vegetables. Rye, wheat, and barley. Rich crops. Sheep, too. We had a school that went through the seventh form and many after-school clubs.

We obtained our food through our labor. In 1930 there were no open labor books. It was the kolkhoz administration that kept their own track of how much people worked. By use of their system, the administration recorded our labor days. But our leader was very good. We trusted him. "Payerovsky" was his family name. I don't remember his first name.

In Sakisky, we built two barns. They were for storing the production of the kolkhoz.

It was a very productive kolkhoz and everyone lived very well. We had electricity, radio, and weekly movies. Nobody starved.

We had some sort of arrangement with the Black Sea Fleet. The fleet always bought vegetables from us.

Yes, everyone lived well. If the war hadn't started, no one would have left the kolkhoz. Life there was really great.

My mother milked thirteen cows by hand, There were no machines so all the milking was by hand. I was nine years old when I learned to milk a cow. At first it was very hard but my mother taught me how to do it and it soon became easier.

My mother went to work at four in the morning. Our family had great cows. Muchnik Paulina was my favorite.

I feel pride as I remember my family, my friends, and my relatives. I really loved my kolkhoz and if there had not been for the war, I would have returned and spent my entire life there. We had people from about thirteen different nationalities. It is very hard for me to understand why there are wars at all, why people fight except to defend themselves.

I disagree with anti-Semitism. In our kolkhoz we always celebrated all holidays from every nationality together at the same time. We were like one big family.

Yes, and we were all very hard working.

Childhood

ANNA ISRAELEVNA

I can tell you about our kolkhoz from when I was a child. I can remember a long time ago, way, way back. I remember my life from the age of five and I am sure of everything from the age of seven on. Whatever I tell you, I can still see as an image before my eyes.

LYUDMILA ALEKSANDROVNA

When I was a child, I read a lot and played with friends. I was like all children. I had a normal childhood until the war ruined it.

I had so many friends. I am a communicative person. I can't remember all that we kids did when we got together. We ran. We swam. We had fun.

My grandmother was from Vienna. She was a really tough woman. She taught us all how to do everything. We made money from knitting clothes for people.

After the war, my sister and I were grateful to Grandma for all the skills she taught us.

LYDYA BORISOVNA

Today, children have too much free time and don't know what to do with themselves. Back then when we had holidays, we worked and helped our families. Five o'clock was when we had to bring cows to the pasture. It was only then that we had free time.

We played games then, many games: Ball-On-A-String. Hide and Seek. We made wreathes from camomile and we put them on cows' tails and that made us laugh and laugh. We had a theater; there is still a Crimean Tatar Theater in our district. We put on beautiful performances. We had a club. We recited poetry. It was all so wonderful. We had a dance hall, too. We performed our traditional dances. Some of us worked hard and helped our parents. But we also had plenty of free time. We made excursions into the town. We had a radio committee. And I wrote a newspaper column about all these things

BORIS GREGORIEVICH

I remember when we were children, we went to synagogue and there we had magnificent dinners and on every holiday the synagogue gave us about 100 rubles.

OLGA SIMONOVNA

My parents worked hard. My mom labored in the field. It was very, very hard work. But she always tried to be the best one. They had a red bulletin board somewhere in the kolkhoz announcing the top workers. She was always one of them, usually the first. So me and my brother, we were little then, and when my mom needed to go to work, she would leave us near the door outside the house. If some of the neighbors would see us sitting near the door, they would shout to her, "*Minya*, your kids are sitting near the door!" And my mom would answer, "Okay! *You* take them to kindergarten! I must go to work!"

Here's another little story: I was very young. We were running away in a cart on one side of a bridge and the Germans were shooting from the plane and the bullets were passing my face. I was almost able to see the flashes. Because I was a kid, I was fascinated by those lights. I wanted to catch them. Fortunately my father got to me just in time to save my life. He wouldn't let me catch bullets.

The Family

ANNA ISRAELEVNA

You want to know about my family? My father was head of the kolkhoz. My mother was in charge of the kindergarten. My oldest sister was an agronomist. She and my third sister were teachers. The youngest was a teenage leader. She didn't have an education because of the work she had to do but, of course, everyone worked very hard in those days.

ASYA MOYESEVOVNA

One day I was in school in the first form and had learned a very long poem because it was the anniversary of the first ten years of the Soviet Union. I headed home and on the way heard someone screaming and crying. I thought it was my sister but it turned out to have been my mother who was crying because she had just received a telegram saying that my father was dead. That was on the sixth of November. The seventh of November was a great Soviet holiday, the victory of the Revolution.

I remember everything.

My father had been the director of a big organization, "Moloko Soyuz," the Milk Union. When Lenin died, my father wept. He was a very emotional man.

In 1927 my father took me to Tsrupinsk for my health. It was by the sea. I was seven.

When my twin brother and sister were born in 1927, my father bought a Primus gas stove in Kharkiv and brought it to the kolkhoz.

It was a wonderful invention. All the neighbors came to see it.

I loved movies. Chapayev was my favorite.

Our family was well off. I was far from being a peasant and my dad was the director of a large organization.

My mother? I am so proud of her. Although she had three children and her husband died, she managed to give me a good secondary education and one of my sisters got to be a teacher but the other one did not like to study at all. My mother worked in the kolkhoz until the war. Then she was evacuated toTashkent with my sisters. They all survived.

My grandfather had lived for a long time in Dobry but then he moved to Nikolaev when collectivization began. He had five sons. In 1914, he built a very large house with ten rooms. It had a white roof. He was a rich man. Then collectivization began and the local Party decided to take over his property to make it part of the kolkhoz. He and his two sons had to move to Nikolaev so as not to be arrested.

My grandmother was very kind. She secretly helped poor people and my grandfather never knew know about it.

My uncle, one of my grandfather's sons, was a Communist and as a result, grandfather disowned him. My father, though, was okay with the Revolution. Nobody in our family was ever arrested. They worked the land and remained in Nikolaev.

The family was okay.

MIKHAIL GREGORIEVICH

My family moved to Nikolaev in 1939. My sister graduated from medical school. During the war she worked in the hospital there. At that time there was permission for the workers at the hospital to go on vacation with their families. So even though the war was going on they all spent the summer in Novorossisk and Machatkala in Dagestan.

ALEKSANDR ZAKHAROVICH

The next year after we arrived, we built a school. We made it from local materials—a certain stone named rakushushnik, meaning "stone made of stone."

Then we organized the school. It was a distinctly Jewish school.

All instruction was in Yiddish. We had one director and one teacher whose name was Samuil Yakovlevitch Brim. I remember him because he always wrote positive comments about me in my note-books. I was a very good student. We studied Yiddish language and literature, Russian language and literature, and mathematics.

School

LYUDMILA ALEKSANDROVNA

Before the war life was good. It was a normal life. I studied in school. I went to a Russian school and my sister went to a Jewish school. The director of the Jewish school suggested to our father that he enroll her in the Russian school because she wrote poems very well in Russian.

I speak German but, my apologies, I am ashamed that I don't speak English.

SOFIA IVANOVNA

We spoke only Yiddish in those days. The school was all in Yiddish. I only learned to speak Russian later when we were evacuated to the Caucasus. I went to a technical school and then graduated from a school that trained construction workers. After that, I graduated in Construction from a correspondence school.

ANNA ISRAELEVNA

In 1925, thirty-six families from the big village of Kalinindorf went to the empty land and built a new community, a little subdivision of the larger village. It was called a *hutor*. It contained several houses. We had a Yiddish name for our hutor, "Rotfeld" or Red Field. It was tiny and had no school. I was only required to attend for the first time at the age of nine. And then I was sent to school in a neighboring hutor, Frifeld, or Free Field, a kilometer and a half away. Later they opened a primary school in Rotfeld and I transferred back.

The Rotfeld school was in a big room in my house. We put four tables there, enough for eight people. We had a kindly teacher, Hava Esther was her name. She told me that someday I would become a teacher, too. And she was right because I did become a teacher.

The language of instruction was Yiddish. I passed seven classes in Yiddish. I also obtained a Yiddish technical school teacher training certificate. It was not until 1939 that it was mandated that all schools were required to function in the Ukrainian language. I have been speaking of the villages at an earlier time when everyone spoke Yiddish.

LISA EFIMOVNA

I went to school in the village of Savaidak where there was a Jewish school that only had four grades. When I finished I went to a school in the village of Yazarey for the fifth form. After that, I went to Ingulets where my uncle lived. I moved in with him and went to the sixth and seventh form there.

After I finished seventh form, I went to Kiev where there was an institute for Jews. I passed my exams and entered the Institute. I finished that technical school and then I enrolled in university to become a teacher.

The university was moved to Odessa. And I moved with it. The whole country needed teachers badly at that time. So the program was accelerated. It was then designed for three years rather than four.

Upon graduation I had to go and work in Kalinindorf, now called Kalininskaya. That was in 1936.

I taught Yiddish language and literature in that school until 1938 when I married a man who was a Jew. We moved to Schandorf, a small place that also had a Jewish school. I worked there until the end of the war.

There was a law in 1938 that allowed teachers to be transferred to a different educational station in order to continue our work there. An examination was required. I was afraid of it but I passed. They checked everything I did, my teaching plans, my diaries and recommendations from members of the department of education.

ASYA MOYESEVOVNA

In the villages, people only spoke Yiddish. I graduated from a Yiddish primary school. Then I came here to Nikolaev and went to a Russian school. Instruction in my medical school was in Russian. After attending the Jewish primary school, I couldn't speak Russian well and couldn't write well either in that language. So I took adult education classes for a year before I was able to enroll in medical school.

When I was a student, I lived with my aunt. The medical school gave my aunt 20 rubles for my room and board. And my mom sent me some food from the kolkhoz so I was able to live quite well. I like to eat and was always able to eat my fill in those days.

LYUDMILA ALEKSANDROVNA

I went to a school in the kolkhoz that had seven forms. From the first through the seventh everything was in Yiddish. The eighth form was in the city and everything there was in Russian. It was very hard for me.

My older brother finished the 7th form in Yiddish. Then my aunt sent him to Kharkiv. She wanted him to have a trade education. But because he knew only Yiddish, he was not eligible for this educational opportunity so my aunt brought him home again. But he had no passport, only a labor book. Life was very difficult for him.

He went back again to school [cries].

He repeated the 7th form. He was very hardworking and talented so he continued on through 7th, 8th, and 9th forms and then went into the army. He was eighteen or nineteen when he served in the Baltic fleet. I had some photos of him … but they were taken away from me.

My brother remained in the Baltic Fleet during the whole war.

By the time I started sixth grade, I could read, write and speak some Russian but I didn't become good in Russian until the eighth form.

Love and Marriage

SOFIA IVANOVNA

My husband was in the army until 1947 when he came back to Crimea and started to study at technical school. Then we got married. We had worked in different places, different organizations. Our son was born in 1952. In 1956, we had our second son; two sons, Sasha and Volodya. They both graduated from construction institutes and they have both worked as engineers and contractors, and they both

live and work in Russia. They are both married and each has a son
and a daughter. One of my granddaughters knows four languages,
Russian, English, French and German and is married. We have no
great grandchildren yet.

ASYA MOYESEVOVNA

I married and lived in Tagonrog. My husband, Simon Gregorievich, was Russian, a sailor. I was afraid of my grandfather because
I was about to marry a Russian. He thought I must only marry a
Jew. My grandfather became so extremely angry that I decided to
leave Nikolaev and settle in Tagonrog.

My husband and I met in Nikolaev. His ship came to the port on
our river. And I fell in love with him.

This is how it happened: I had enrolled in a dance course. We
learned the tango, fox-trot and waltz. Simon took the course, too, and
it was there that we noticed each other. We never danced together
then. But I watched him and noticed that he didn't have a girlfriend.
We finally met in 1939 after two or three years. He was a very fine,
honest, well-educated man. He read a lot and was always very interesting to talk with.

We wrote letters to each other when the war came. When he was
demobilized, he was sent to Kokomna near Moscow but he did not
have a flat to live in so he decided to come to Tagonrog to stay with
his relatives. He took me with him. We could have lived together in
Nikolaev but as I said, I was afraid of my grandfather.

My grandfather was very honest man, a very strong man. He
would say, "I am honest so I must tell you: I don't believe you!" He
put it that way instead of saying simply, "You lie!"

BORIS GREGORIEVICH

My cousin married a German woman. Five days after the marriage, the war began and I went into the army. This German girl was
evacuated with my mother, my brothers, and sisters to Uzbekistan.
She went along with them and waited for him. Eventually, they all
returned home to Dobry. The Germans who were in Dobry retreated
to Germany taking my cousin with them as a prisoner.

For ten years, my cousin tried to find the German girl. And she
tried to find him. He finally gave up and got married again and had a

child with his new wife. It was then that she returned to Nikolaev and finally found him but with a new family. He offered to abandon that family and live with her but she declined saying that a man must stay with his wife and child.

ANNA IOSIFOVNA (RUSSIAN)/HANNAH SHIFREH (YIDDISH NAME)

I got married when I returned to the kolkhoz. I was a *Komsomol* member assigned to the district office. I worked there for a year but wanted to go back to school. 1n 1945, I went to Simferopol to study at the construction institute.

That's where I met my husband. The war was over. He had been in the military. He was twenty-seven; I was twenty-three. And in 1946, we got married. I finished the institute and had a specialization.

My husband and I had been acquainted for a long time. His parents helped our family get to Armenia. After the war, my husband's family returned but I didn't know where.

We had a son. He had a diploma in construction. He went to the army and he ... [cries] ... in 1988 my husband and my son both died. My mother-in-law lived with us for 32 years. My son was 31 when he died.…[weeps].

I don't want to talk about it.

LYUDMILA ALEKSANDROVNA

My girlfriends and I laughed all the time. I met my husband in school. My future husband and his friends noticed and said about me, "She always laughs."

Another guy walked me home every evening. School lasted until eleven at night. One evening, my future husband asked to take me home. I answered that the road is plenty wide—so come join us! From that time on, my future husband did not let anyone take me home except him. It was his job. Only for him.

We were in a relationship for a year and then we got married. I was 26. At first my mother was against it. She wanted me to marry a Jewish guy. My boyfriend was Russian. But fortunately it turned out to be okay with my mother. She loved him right away when she met him.

There was one family in our neighborhood who were on vacation.

They were really wealthy. When they returned, the mother of the family wanted me to marry her son. We were very poor so my mother was thinking that it might be good for me to marry that guy just for his money. My boyfriend's family were as poor as we were although they had many skills.

I just didn't like that other guy. I don't like people who think they are so great. On the other hand, they were making good money. They were a family of photographers.

My husband wasn't exactly Russian. His family came from Latvia; Poland and France, too. His family was quite a mix of nationalities.

Well, my mother changed her mind and my marriage turned out to be a very good one. My husband always came to the family with a gift. And my mother really accepted him. The only thing was that Yiddish was spoken in our home and languages were a bit of a problem for him. My husband was always asking, "What did he say? What did she say?"

My mother once told him, "So many years have past. Why haven't you learned Yiddish already?"

We lived together for fifty-two years. We have two children, a daughter and a son and four grandchildren. One grandchild died in an automobile accident.

Looking back I can say that my life was really calm and wonderful. My husband didn't drink. And he didn't smoke either. It was a happy life.

The Job

LYUDMILA ALEKSANDROVNA

I finished school and then I found work in finance. My sister became a bookkeeper.

I didn't work in the kolkhoz. I am an economist. I completed my training in a school for builders—like a high school. And then I got into an economics institute and increased my qualifications. Next I found a job in a shoe factory and finally got transferred to a plastic factory. The work was good. I received honors. The director of the factory and I got along very well.

SOFIA IVANOVNA

I worked in different regions and in different cities. I was an engineer for ten years at one of the institutes and for eighteen years I worked in one of the Simferopol construction organizations. Then for twenty-five years I was employed by a government organization that supplied heating equipment and installed heating systems.

I had wanted to become a doctor when I was little. I always liked to help people. But I couldn't go to medical school because it was expensive. Not the tuition—that was free—but students needed to pay for living expenses. If I had gone to medical school, I would have needed to study and would also have had to find time to work and receive a salary. It would have been impossible. But in technical school I was able to work and support myself, too.

YFIM GREGORIEVICH

I went to school in Kherson. Everything was good. I played football. I joined the culture club. It was good after the war, too. I was a sea man on a merchant ship. I studied at first after school and, after the war, I studied at the Marine School and after that I sailed on merchant ships. I got to America and Cuba. A great life. Everything was beautiful. Spain: wonderful. Singapore, too.

ANNA ISRAELEVNA

I worked in Kherson as a teacher with little children for 27 years. When I was required to teach in the Ukrainian language, I did so but I had Yiddish accent.

I received many medals for my work.

Students still come to see me. They are now over 70 years old. They celebrate my birthday. When I was ninety, 90 of my students came to me to celebrate.

LYDYA BORISOVNA

After I completed the 10th form, I received the diploma and I was assigned to the Bulgaraki Oblast where I joined a collective farm now called Vinogradny. I told my parents that I would work there for two years and then enter the medical university here in Simferopol.

I was assigned to the hospital where I worked and took courses and learned about many different aspects of medicine. Many people from the kolkhozy were treated there.

I completed three years in the nurses' training program and received my diploma. I then decided to increase my skills as a nurse by entering Crimea Medical University.

ASYA MOYESEVOVNA

I moved to Nikolaev and eventually went to medical school. I worked as a paranatal doctor and continued in that profession for 45 years. All told, I worked for 52 years, total. That is a long work life for this country. I retired when I was 72 because I had problems with my ears.

Throughout my professional life, I have always wanted to be useful. At first, however, it was frustrating because I was inexperienced and necessarily marginal. I was afraid I was a bother and that the head doctor would just tell me to go away.

Many children, Jewish children, left the kolkhoz and went to the nearest towns because they could earn a real salary there. At the same time, there were many ethnic German people in the village who worked in our kolkhoz.

Why did I become a doctor? Well, all of my friends went to the Pedagogical Institute and became teachers. But, frankly, I never liked children. The only other opportunities for a person like me was to become an engineer or a doctor and I had no interest in engineering. So, becoming a doctor was inevitable.

I was not actually a doctor but was rather someone between a nurse and a physician. I could have gone to Odessa to complete my medical training and become a full-fledged doctor but I was afraid of the famine there. There was more food security in Nikolaev.

I only treated women, not men. When a woman cries and then gives birth and then she smiles, that was the most satisfying part of my work.

LYUDMILA ALEKSANDROVNA

When I was a little girl, my father and I were carrying water from the village pump in pails. My water spilled but his did not. He was skilled because as a little boy, his job was to bring water to rich people who would give him money. Before industrialization, he was a student of metal work and later became a professional metal worker. The person he worked for was a famous Jew, the founder of a big factory. "Gourevitch" was the man's name. The Soviet government appropriated the plant but Gourevitch continued to run it and my father continued to work for him.

When the First World War began, my father was 18 and joined the army. Everyone wanted to be a pilot at that time and he did, too, but he already had a profession, two of them. He was a master metal worker and a mechanic as well. The Soviets would not send him to school to be a pilot. That would be a third profession, an unnecessary governmental expense.

During the war we lived under the bridge in the Kalininskaya Oblast. My father was stationed at the military aerodrome.

He stayed in the army for 26 years.

ANNA IOSIFOVNA (RUSSIAN)/HANNAH SHIFREH (YIDDISH)

I didn't even know what a Pioneer Camp was. My whole life was work. I finished school and then worked in the kolkhoz because I knew I had to have the labor book with enough credit because we all needed to eat. I worked with pigs with my grandfather. With my mother, I worked with calves.

I worked in the grape orchard and I worked hard, very hard, even on holidays. I worked after school and on vacations.

After the 8th form, I returned to the kolkhoz on holidays and worked some more. The kolkhoz had a collective kitchen. I had my own horse. The kolkhoz gave me that horse and a cart so I could bring food to the collective.

I did all sorts of hard things with the horse. I rode it. That was too hard for a little girl but I did it anyway. I put the tack on. That was hard, too, but I did it.

I would come to the collective kitchen on my horse and was given food that I brought out to the field to feed the workers.

Then afterward I would clean up the kitchen. This was during the summer break. Some of the girls were rich. Rich children did not work. Poor children worked. There were not so many children who worked as hard as I did.

There was another girl who was older than me and she and I had the same job but had another wagon. While we poor girls worked, the rich girls mostly just hung around at home.

OLGA SIMONOVNA

When I was maybe five years old, I remember there was no work for women during the wintertime so they organized a hat-making workshop. Agro-Joint would send raffia for them to make those hats. I was a kid and I always liked to do something with my hands. So I remember that I was there at that workshop helping women make hats, sew hats and knit hats. I liked it a lot so every woman would ask me to help them thread the needle because my eyes were good. They would say, "*Olichka*! Come and help me get started!"

I was able to earn some money by working there so my mom bought me two dresses for school.

Even to this day I like to sew and knit. I worked as a seamstress for 40 years. I like it still, even now.

When I turned 16, we were living in East Kazakhstan. I obtained an internal passport, a very valuable document. The day after I got it, I heard from a man in authority. He said, "Do you want to study?" I answered, "Yes. I want to become a seamstress." He said, "I will send you to Karaganda."

That official was supposed to send me there, far away from home, to study. But he took my internal passport. So when I went home and told my mom that I was going off to study, my mom started to cry. And when I came to work, I saw my friend, actually she was a Jewish friend of my mom's, and told her that I was going to Karaganda,

The Jewish friend of my mom said to my mom, "Why didn't you come to my husband before talking to that person? We will help you buy your daughter back from being sent to Karaganda and we will make sure that she gets her passport back." So my parents gave her some money and she bought me out of that Karaganda trip and I stayed with my parents in the city and found a job there.

SOFIA IVANOVNA

Families used to live a couple of families in one big room. Kids used to study and during the summer, we worked helping to harvest vegetables and fruits. All us kids worked. No one was forced to; there was so much patriotism. People would rush off in the mornings to do their jobs. They would take their bicycles and ride to the fields. There was a very high spirit of citizenship. People would take a twelve kilometer ride on a bike from the field to their home to milk a cow and immediately bike back to the field.

I don't remember much from when I was a child. But I know that I was always a very communicative person.

Back in the 1930s, we had everything. There was no such thing as scraping "to survive." My parents worked in the kolkhoz and we had all that we needed. Everything: food, a place to live. Everything. But things changed during the war. Ukrainians came to live in the kolkhozy. Our kolkhoz became not just Jewish but included people from all other nationalities. Anybody you wanted, you could find there.

A Good Life

ASYA MOYESEVOVNA

I had a good life in the kolkhoz. I played *football* and went to the movies. And I had lots of friends—especially boys. In 1934, the kolkhoz sent a group of us kids to Odessa to the theater, the opera. We heard Otello. I remember it so well. It was wonderful. We ate olives when we were in Odessa. Odessa was more civilized than Nikolaev. Odessa had an opera theater and we didn't. But Nikolaev wasn't so bad. We had a Russian dramatic theater there beginning in 1935. I went to the theater as often as I could, maybe once a month; the Nikolaev United Theater. I don't remember if there was Yiddish theater in Nikolaev then.

ANNA IOSIFOVNA (RUSSIAN)/HANNAH SHIFREH (YIDDISH)

I had no notebooks. I wrote everything between the lines of my old books. I had one friend, Sonya, from a Yiddish family but she was rich. I asked Sonya to give me a book to read. In return Sonya told me to clean her floor. I never told this story to anybody. [Weeps].

There were poor people in the kolkhoz and there were rich people. We had five children in my family. We were poor and there wasn't ever enough to eat. It was too much for me. I didn't understand what to do but I knew I had to work and work and work to eat and to help my family.

I had friends including a German girl. The kolkhoz became big and after a while not everybody was Jewish. My German friend taught me to knit and now I am a great knitter. I was very capable and always loved to do anything.

This girl was my only entertainment. We would meet and study together. There were a lot of Russians in our school, too. When the teaching was in Russian, a lot of kids from the area would come.

It wasn't important if a person was Russian or Jewish or German.

Immersed in Events
ALEKSANDR ZAKHAROVICH

Our kolkhoz was created by Stalin. Some people blame him for our hunger but that had nothing to do with his policies. The starvation, which was more severe in Ukraine than in Crimea, was the result of a terrible drought as well as the rapid pace of collectivization.

Hunger wasn't only in Ukraine. The claim that only Ukraine was affected is just politics.

YELENA GERSHMANOVNA

No matter what anybody says about the famine, it was not a political act. It was caused by the dryness of the land. That was a really hard time; 1933, a very difficult year.

LYUDMILA ALEKSANDROVNA

The entire Agro-Joint program was stopped by Stalin. This was very unfair because Joint had done such good work here. Stalin was a terrible man. Can you imagine? He was in seminary to become a priest but he became an executioner instead.

Anti-Semitism and Identity
SOFIA IVANOVNA

The Soviet government never helped us at all. It was only Agro-Joint.

We were mostly patriotic to the Jewish community, not so much to the Soviet Union. On the other hand, we also did have some feeling for the USSR. My aunt was given a medal from the government for her work achievements.

At first we didn't have much interest in Israel but eventually we had a desire to find out more about that new country. But at the same time, we were assimilating quickly in the Soviet Union. We began marrying Russians and at the same time many people were emigrating to other countries and moving to areas of this country that had once been forbidden to us.

Some of my own family moved to Israel and elsewhere. I am now alone here in Crimea. Everyone has moved. My children are in Russia because my son went to study in St. Petersburg after the USSR collapsed. Most of my family is in Russia and here I am alone in Crimea.

After the Revolution most people wanted to remain in the Soviet Union. Suddenly there was no anti-Semitism. We had some non-Jews in our kolkhoz but since we lived together, it didn't matter who was Jewish and who was not.

After the *Great Patriotic War*, Jews were once more discriminated against. We could not get jobs or we were not allowed to study.

I don't know personally about Stalin's hostility to Agro-Joint and his killing of the leadership. Maybe it is true. I think it probably happened. We had so much support in the 1920s and in the 1930s suddenly it stopped. Then there was the Doctors' Plot. I don't know the details but I do know that there were persecutions. Jews pretended that they were not Jews. They were scared. My father was Belarusian. I would tell people that my nationality is Russian. People would say, "But you have a Jewish face."

After the war, I worked as a housekeeper in the home of a Communist party leader. The name of that family was Solivov. He was taken to prison because he was accused of working for the Americans. I also worked for another family who were taken to Siberia.

The second family, their name was Chursin. I spent more time working for them. I believe that the father was shot. After a time, the family came back but the father never did. Because of this, I think he was shot.

What did I think about politics? I didn't have much understanding. I had sympathy for the Soviet government. But I also had sympathy for the people I worked for who were accused. I didn't believe that they were spies. They treated me so well. I didn't know much about their lives.

My husband, Volodya, was not Jewish. His mother was German and his father was Russian. When Volodya was 17 years old, he ran away to the army. Then his family was arrested and sent to Siberia. That was because his mother was German. Of course they had no relation to the Nazis.

Who knows what to think about such things? Politics were like that at the time.

YFIM GREGORIEVICH

I was born 2 March, 1925, in Kherson City, not in a settlement. There were no trolleybuses at the time. There were about 100,000 citizens of which about 8,000 or 10,000 were Jews. There were a lot of jobs and new organizations. Factories were springing up. There was famine in 1931 but we had help from Agro-Joint. In the villages, the government took everything from the people and didn't give them any help because they wanted to force people to join kolkhozy.

Many, many people died in the villages. But in the city, there was help from the Joint so people stayed alive.

It was a part of history that after the civil war, there were no jobs. That meant there was no food. But with the *New Economic Policy,* the NEP, it became better. New stores opened and there were new possibilities. A lot of jobs appeared but after the NEP ended, hunger returned once again; no jobs, no food.

By the middle of the 1930s, an industrialization process began and the government stepped away from being so hard in pushing for collectivization. By 1935, people could come to the cities to work in industry. In the cities, you had to have an internal passport but in the kolkhozy, you were required to give up your passport. That meant you could not move. They started taking the passports away from us right before the war but before that, people could leave and they did. During the war, if you didn't have a passport you could not go anywhere.

And if you were a kulak, if you wanted a slave, if you exploited other people, the government would send you to Siberia. If you made jokes, you could be sent to prison. In the 1930s, a lot of people were deported to Siberia but when the war started, people in trouble with the government were sent to war.

ANNA ISRAELEVNA

In fact, there was friendship between the communities—Jewish and Ukrainian. And there was no antisemitism. We were like one family. It was good for me and for everyone. It continued to be a good thing until 1991. That was the end of the Soviet Union. Then came hate, to Jews and to everyone. Our country became evil. I don't feel safe on the streets anymore. There is a new wave of anti-Semitism here in Kherson.

The problem is political.

It used to be better. People became rich then but remained friendly as the kolkhozy developed. There were no bosses; no millionaires. People worked together.

LYDYA BORISOVNA

You want to know if I am interested in Israel? Well, I was excited by it at first. But then I read that 300,000 non-Jews live there and that they are disappointed in Israel and things about it. I read this in the newspaper. Some engineer from Beersheva wrote that there was some disorder. I don't want to move to Israel or anyplace else now anyway because I am 87.

ASYA MOYESEVOVNA

I don't go to the Jewish Community Center. I don't like it there because they always talk politics, Ukrainian politics. I don't like politics. I prefer to read; classic books, magazines but not newspapers except for maybe once a week.

But I sometimes read newspapers about proposals for pension reform legislation. These are horrible ideas because if they go through, retired people will have to pay for support. I have such a good son-in-law. He says, "Don't read such terrible things! You have a family. We will always help you."

SOFIA IVANOVNA

People in the Caucasus would rub our heads looking for horns. They would say, "On Jewish heads there are horns and that's why you should be afraid of Jews." I remember if they saw a Jew on the street, they would yell, "Hate a Jew and save Russia!" They screamed those words and threw sticks at us with pins on the ends.

While adults were at work or at home, local kids would bother us. But this was just kids being mean to kids.

The older I get, the more connected I feel to Jewishness, the more Jewish I feel especially after I lost my husband and was left alone. The khesed included me and helped me feel part of the Jewish community.

My grandchildren don't feel Jewish. It is only my younger son who feels somewhat connected to Jewishness.

There was a lot of persecution of Jews before the war and during the war and especially after the war. It's funny when I get together with my Russian women friends. Whenever we tell a joke or a story where a Jew is a character, everybody looks at me because I am the only Jew in the group. But I don't feel any judgement from them.

I have a feeling of gratitude toward Israel because many of my relatives are there and they live very well. They are all rich; they all graduated from university and one even works as a doctor there.

I want there to be peace in the Middle East. I don't want war. I want people to be friendly to one another. We have been taught that Palestinians and Jews are related so why would they want to have a war? That's what I know according to the Bible. I don't know personally if we are relatives or not but that is what the Bible says. It is a pity that they cannot come to a mutual understanding.

I used to go to the Baptist church and study the Bible with them. One of my friends is a Baptist and she attends their church. I went with her a couple of times but I don't go there anymore.

Baptists are more supportive of Jews than the Russian Orthodox people. The Apostle Paul wrote to Jews. So whenever the church writes verses about Jews, my Baptist friend calls me and says, "Read that verse! It is good! It is about Jews!"

YFIM GREGORIEVICH

When I was a child, there were no such thing as a "Jewish community." Everyone was a Soviet citizen. But our parents always talked with each other in Yiddish.

LYUDMILA ALEKSANDROVNA

My father used to say, "I am Jewish according to my internal passport but my language is Russian." He actually knew Yiddish very well, too.

The fact that he knew Yiddish so well made it possible for him to understand German. too. When the war ended, he again worked in the plant. My mother was very ill then but she also worked at the factory. And there were German prisoners of war who were forced to remain here and they worked in the plant as well. Because he could understand German, my father took leadership of the factory team.

The Germans were put to work building houses. My father was in charge of them.

Stalin put an end to the kolkhozy. He was more interested in industrialization. Was that influenced by his anti-Semitism? I can't say. But I don't think that there were obvious signs of anti-Semitism in Stalin at that time.

In the 1930s my father went to a Jewish school. The language of instruction was Yiddish so anti-Semitism was not apparent to any of us until after the war just before Stalin died.

Hunger

ALEKSANDR ZAKHAROVICH

In 1932, 1933, and 1934, famine hit our area. I remember my father had a wedding ring that he sold to get food. We used sunflower oil to make animal feed; people would eat it as well.

ANNA ISRAELEVNA

Famines—how did we get through them? During the famine of 1921 and 1922, it was very hard but there were few deaths in our community. Everybody managed to find a little something, maybe a sauce of bread. In the spring, we used a grass, "labadar," and anything else we could find. Horses were dying because of the famine. Cows, too. There were a lot of vitamins in labadar so we did get through. But nobody helped the villages. People had nothing. We have a saying, "With a lot of holes, you can't make anything except a big hole."

The famines of 1932, 1933, and 1937 were different. They were during the time of the kolkhozy. In our kolkhoz it was not so bad because we had a system that preserved our seed. We put the seed aside and we traded only the previous year's crops. This system helped us survive. We were wise enough by then. It was hard but ... nobody died.

Jews are clever. We don't live one day at a time. We plan. We think. Nobody died in 1933. That's a fact. Our region was Jewish. Ukrainians suffered far more but there was no hatred between the two groups.

ASYA MOYESEVOVNA

I myself never worked in the kolkhoz, but my mother did. My mother was very well trained in agriculture so we had no problems with food. In 1933, people suffered from famine but no one in my village died. We didn't receive money from the state or from the outside. We survived on our own. No one died but we were very poor. We had only one cow.

The Ukrainian kolkhozy were even poorer. And many of their people did die.

MIKHAIL GREGORIEVICH

We were boys and we helped our parents and we helped the kolkhoz and we always had food. We helped to gather grapes and we ate them as we picked them.

We never experienced a famine.

But there was a bad famine in Nikolaev among the Ukrainians. Our people had work to do. Ours was a small town and there were a lot of people who knew how to repair things.

Before the war there were only small houses. After the war we began to build big houses.

In 1932 and 1933 the harvests were very bad, especially for the Ukrainians.

There was no famine in the Jewish kolkhozy. Even the Ukrainians who lived near us didn't experience a famine. We helped them and they gave us cars, trucks, and even trains to help us evacuate to the east.

LYUDMILA ALEKSANDROVNA

In my family there was my grandma on my father's side, my mother, father, and eight children. They arrived in the Kherson oblast during the first famine and when it subsided, they went on to another city, Delnitsa.

This was in 1921. Two of my father's brothers starved to death.

The famine of 1921 was due to natural causes such as an extraordinary drought. But in 1931 there was another famine, a fake once caused by Stalin's policies.

There was a program to save the children in 1921, a program only for children. It found food for them. It also taught them to read. ASARCO was what the program was called. Herbert Hoover later became president of the United States. ASARCO sent Agro-Joint to save the children here. Lenin asked them to come and they did.

Children ate in our kolkhoz but they were not allowed to take anything out of the dining hall. So they would hide cornbread rolled into little pieces on their bodies. They would sneak them out to bring to their parents to keep them from starving. A terrible story.

OLGA SIMONOVNA

Once my mom got very sick because of the famine. We had only water and salt at home. Our neighbor came by and suggested that I work at the basement of the train station sorting potatoes. When I got there, the owner of the basement learned about our situation and my sick mom and he gave me eight big potatoes. I took them home, boiled them, and fed my mom and as a result, she stayed alive. I was fourteen at the time.

When we were in the Pavlogradskaya region, it was very cold because it was winter and I remember we lived in a small building, a tiny room in the kolkhoz. My mom was working so hard. She got to be the best worker and she received the prize which was a little pig. That pig kept us alive.

Cataclysm

ALEKSANDR ZAKHAROVICH

In 1941, my brother joined the army. He was in a battalion.

The year 1941 was a good year for cultivation. We didn't think that the war would reach here in Simferopol. At first it was calm. Then we heard that the Nazis had invaded Russia. We tried to evacuate people, animals, and material. One hundred sixty people went to Kerch because Kerch belonged to Russia rather than Ukraine.

But some Jewish people decided to stay right where they were.

One man, Aaron Zelichovik, said, "Why are you so worried about German people? They are excellent farmers and good neighbors. They will not harm us."

Aaron Zelichovik was murdered there, too, along with his wife.

Some of us actually welcomed the German army and we lived in a kind of peace with them for a month and a half. Then they received an order to gather all the Jews in front of the school. They assembled 84 people and marched them to the railway station where they shot them all.

Not many Jewish people survived. I myself survived only because I was not there. My family had evacuated early. I was in Baku at the time I am talking about. I heard about what happened after the war was over.

It was only chance, accidental good fortune, that my mother and I remained alive. My mother became very sick with malaria at that time.

Like my brother, I joined the army. I wanted to fight.

LYUDMILA ALEKSANDROVNA

The war was a scary time. We didn't understand the whole situation. The place where we were living was near the airport. There were lots of German planes flying around above us. We had to hide almost every day. It was very scary.

But we lived a long time. My husband died in 2005. He died in hospital of a heart attack. His heart just stopped.

ANNA ISRAELEVNA

We lost our father at the start of the war as we evacuated. He was killed by a bomb fragment. Some soldiers helped me bury him. After the war I returned to where he was buried but we could not find the site. It had become a road.

All the husbands went to the war and all of them were killed.

I had a brother. He was a pilot and in one battle he shot down two German planes but the third shot him down. This took place over Kharkiv. As he was hit, he saw a train loaded with German equipment and he flew his plane right into it and blew it up. First he told his mechanic to jump and live to tell his family how he died. This man did survive and he sent us a letter.

[She bursts into tears.]

My sister's husband survived. They had been married for only one year when she became pregnant. Her baby was born right before the war and was one and a half years old at the time of evacuation. Her husband became very ill. They could not find medication for him so he became thinner and thinner. But somehow they saved him. My sister said, "You will live for a long time. We saved you so you will live for a long, long time." It was true. He is still alive today. But he is very old and sick.

Before the war we lived calmly and well. But on August 12th, the Nazi army arrived. We abandoned our homes and evacuated. But some people stayed.

By the middle of September, everyone who remained in the village had been killed.

[Weeps.]

The Nazis took only the Jews. Eighteen hundred and seventy-five Jews were killed in Kalininskaya. It was terrible. The Nazis locked people in barns and set them on fire. Children were inside. Many. Many children. Lots of people were shot or driven to the well and drowned.

LISA EFIMOVNA

My husband had a higher education. He was an animal technician. When the war broke out he took the animals deep into the countryside. Women in the village worked on making tracks for tanks. The crop was good that year. The women had to harvest the crops because the men were in the army. Everyone worked hard. Very hard.

Before the war began, we knew that something was about to happen but our area was not yet a battlefield. While my husband was taking the animals away, I harvested the crops. I helped people from Moldova and Poland evacuate toward the East.

When my husband returned, we held a very important meeting. We women were waiting to find out what we should do. My husband said, "The Germans have been stopped so we must remain where we are. We should not go anywhere." That was the message of this meeting.

An agricultural expert was in our village at that time. This man did not agree with my husband. One night he was on guard. Suddenly he knocked on everybody's door and shouted they must evacuate at once because bombs were falling.

So we ran, me, my husband, our son, my husband's parents, and a little girl, somebody's grandchild maybe from another family. The agriculturalist and his family also ran. Soon we came to a river crossing where my husband had worked some time ago.

Surprising to me was that kids came running around us yelling "Yids! Yids!" I had never heard such a thing before.

When we came to cross the river, the Dniepr, we were stopped because the people who had arranged for the crossing said that the Germans had been stopped at Nikolaev and that it was no longer necessary to evacuate. But because my husband knew all the people around there since he had just negotiated the hiding of the animals, we were permitted to cross and came to a field on the other side. We sat down to consider our situation. We had no idea what to do next.

This agricultural technician had hidden the horses. He thought that the Soviet military would take them to use in the war that he could see was coming. Instead, he brought them out for us. There were three beautiful horses and one of them was white. He understood that it might be a good idea to have horses available very soon.

In the beginning we were a big group, my husband's family with two parents, a son—which was his from a former marriage—and our daughter, his and mine.

Meanwhile, my husband's sister decided to visit my husband in Kalininskaya. When she arrived there, we had already moved out. So she decided to run after us. By the time she got to the river crossing, we had already passed it but she told another family about to cross to tell us that she would be waiting there for us. We received the message. So my husband and my father-in-law took two horses and went back to the west bank. I was left with my mother-in-law and two children. All of this was happening on the 9th of August, 1941.

It was a horrible night because the men were trying to get to my sister-in-law. Suddenly there was a bomb attack and a battle in the sky and nobody knew what to do, how to save themselves. One of the horses was white and was visible at night. People yelled at me to hide that horse because it could be seen. And the children were sleeping on white sheets that were also visible. They also had to hide.

When the battle in the sky was over, people came out from their hiding places. They found a terrible scene, many dead bodies and awful weeping. And on top of it all, I had a problem with my voice because I was so afraid. I could not speak. I had no voice at all because I was paralyzed with fear knowing that we had been surrounded.

But it worked out well. Eventually we were all safely reunited. My husband and father-in-law found my sister-in-law and her family and they all found us again.

LYDYA BORISOVNA

When the war began, the kolkhoz administration selected a leadership group. My father was in that group. We had to evacuate the people; and everything in our community that was valuable had to be hidden from the Germans.

At about the time that I finished the eighth, ninth and tenth forms there was a decision made that each of us was to learn a military skill.

The milkmaids were gathered in one place and told that all the people and cattle were to be evacuated at the same time.

But there was no truck to help with the moving so the milkmaids had to walk the cows along with them. We did have a two wheel cart for use with a horse and that helped a little. The milkmaids went by majara—a high-walled vehicle; sort of a cart. They loaded it with beds and a lot of straw and hay. Horses pulled this contraption, too.

We each had skills. One of my friends knew about airplanes. Another friend was a navigator. Still another was a signalman. I was a nurse.

Many of us were killed. In our tenth form we were 23 children. After the war only two of us returned alive.

One day, Soviet District Infantry Regiment number 397 arrived at the hospital. They were given two rooms to treat soldiers.

On June 21st, 1941, my father came to see me. He wanted to make sure that my living circumstances were good. He was satisfied with all that he saw. But the next morning as the sun rose, we heard a lot of firing, explosions, and all sorts of loud noises. The war had begun. The director of the hospital told people to come get their relatives and go home.

My father returned home with me and then he left. I never saw him again.

On the 24th of June I was officially listed as a member of the regiment and remained with it from then on. I got sent along to Perked with the soldiers. We went to a lake called, "Sivash,"[9] It was there that my military work really began.

I worked of course as a nurse.

[Weeps] In Perekop there were many bloody incidents with the enemy.

[Weeps] From Perekop we moved to the Krasnosavodsky oblast. There were a lot of people stationed there. I was wounded in the city of Bataisk. But I participated in the battles for Novorossisk. Our regiment took refuge during these battles in a cement plant called Oktyber.

I also participated in the battles for Kiev.

There were a great number of battles. We even went beyond the border of Poland. But in Poland there was a law that we were to remain in the railroad car.

From the night of the 5th through the 6th of November, 1943, we were engaged in a battle for the Dniepr. We entered Kiev and then from Kiev we were sent to the northern Caucasus.

We had a lot of guns. After Germany surrendered, these guns were taken to the Far East when the war with the Japanese began. And then on to the Kurilsky Islands.

[Cries] My father was going to bring valuables from the kolkhoz to another place to keep the Germans from getting them but he didn't have much time to do it. He was unable to complete the task because the Germans found him and killed him. He could have survived.

My mother was a milkmaid and brought along the cows when we

9. "The Rotten Sea" in English.

were evacuated. She saw grinning Germans saying, "We will bomb you." And they did but she survived with the other milkmaids by hiding in the reeds. They were almost naked. People helped them. They gave them old clothes. The area was controlled by the Germans who decided that they needed the milkmaids and made them work for them, milking our own cows. They didn't allow them to return to their native kolkhoz but placed them somewhere else. I don't know where.

ASYA MOYESEVOVNA

Later during the war 600 people died in my village. That was out of a total of over 1,000. After the war, the survivors gathered monthly at a monument they built for those people.

Near Dobry there were several Russian villages including Yavkino and Novo Yegorovka. The Jewish villages were Dobri Novopoltavka, and Efimgar—that was its old name. Now it is called Lushinkov. There were a lot of Jewish people in Beleznegovatoye, too Everyone got killed.

It was August, 1941. My mom, my sisters, my aunt and her husband plus their son came to Tagonrog. My mother had lived with German people in Dobry. The family said, "Stay in Dobry!" But mom was in a panic because a lot of Jewish people came from Bessarabia and Moldava to report that Jewish people were being killed everywhere. So my mother said, "Let's go to Tashkent!"

And off we went. We walked the entire distance ... many, many kilometers all across Ukraine to near Rostov and the Sea of Azov. We were dirty and tired.

We decided to go to Tashkent because the German soldiers were coming through Ukraine. But I didn't want to join my family. I was pregnant and I wanted to stay near my husband. He was a master of his trade working in a factory in Tagonrog.

Then he went into the army and I remained in Tagonrog. There was one ship for those who wanted to leave but there were too many people. So we all stayed.

My son was born on the 28th of January, 1942. I did not go to hospital.

LYUDMILA ALEKSANDROVNA

I had an uncle. Yuda was his name. In Soviet times, they called him "Yura." He died in the war.

OLGA SIMONOVNA

When I was 13 years old I helped my family escape from the Germans. I was so brave. We fled through the forest. But we didn't understand what it meant to be Jewish then. That was 1942.

ALEKSANDR ZAKHAROVICH

In 1937 my father became ill. There were no doctors and the nearest hospital was four kilometers away in an ethnic German settlement called Naiman, "New Person" in Yiddish. The doctor there couldn't find the problem and in two weeks my father's condition became very serious. He had no choice but to remain at home.

We finally arranged transportation to get him to hospital in Simferopol. But just as my father was getting in the car, he collapsed and died of an aortic aneurism.

SOFIA IVANOVNA

There were five children in my family. All but me died during the war. Two were shot and two died from illness.

"God always protects her"

ASYA MOYESEVOVNA

People used to say about me, "God always protects her."

I'll give you an example: My husband was very interested in new technology, machinery and so on. He got me a wonderful hand-powered mincing machine—a mill. All the neighbors came to my house to use it. But one of them took the machine and wouldn't give it back. She said she needed it and that other people needed it, too. I said, "NO!" She called me a dirty Jew and grabbed it. We had a big squabble. Well, that woman died in 1944 because she stole something in a train and people beat her to death. My conclusion: "Don't say bad words about Jewish people!"

When some guy yelled at me "You are a Jew! I will kill you!" and threatened to go to the police to report me, well that fellow got killed in an automobile accident.

Another story: In the hospital, a nurse accused me. "You are Jewish!" she said. Well, she had a lot of problems later with her sons and her grandsons.

A bomb once landed near our house. It didn't explode but it was very scary. An Orthodox priest lived in our house. He said, "Don't touch that bomb because Jesus Christ was Jewish and we are all asking him for help right now. Please, Jesus, don't touch Asya." So, I remained safe.

I lived through 1942 and 1943 and nobody touched me and it was okay even though I was Jewish.

Until May, 1945, I didn't tell anybody that I was Jewish. It was only on the 9th of May that my Jewishness became known. That was when the American soldiers issued me a passport on which was written my correct name.

The soldiers gave us a truck and this truck took us back to our homes in Nikolaev. The American soldiers were so good!

Novopoltavka
MARIA IVANOVA A.K.A. MASHA MOISHEMOSHEVNA

My name was originally a Jewish name, Masha Moishemo-shevna. I was born 16 September,1937, here in Novopoltavka. The old name of our kolkhoz was Roeter Oktyabr, Yiddish for Red October. We lived in Novopoltavka and worked here in the kolkhoz. When the war began, all the Jews were put in the pit and shot or they were drowned in the well. People could hear their screams and cries for days. I escaped because my mother changed my name to Maria Ivanova, a Russian name.

Before the war there were only four Russians here and the rest were Jews, maybe a thousand. Now my husband and I are the only Jews and there are maybe a thousand Russians.

The Germans not only said to the Jews, "Go to the well!" They also forced the Russian families to watch what was going on. My mother was Russian. But my father was Jewish. I thought that I was Jewish. I was a little girl and had to run with all the Jews to the well but as I ran, one of the policemen—who was a Russian—decided to save me. He whispered in my ear, "You are a Russian girl!" He told me to hide behind the Russian families who were standing and watching the people drown.

But it was still not safe because the neighbors might say that I was a Jew. That's why I didn't go back home with my mother. Instead I went to my aunt in the next village. She had two boys, my cousins. I spent the night there.

In the morning, the Germans came in my aunt's house. My cousins hid me under their legs in the bed. The Germans said, "If you are hiding any Jews, we will kill you!" But I survived. I think I was the smallest child in the village. That's why I survived. Nobody told on me.

But it was still a very unsafe place to be. It was decided that I should go and live in the *dietsky dom* with new documents.

The policeman made new documents for me using my Russian name, Prachotina Maria Ivanovna. I lived with that name until 1949. Then I changed it back to my real name, my Jewish name.

Years later I needed the help that the government gave to people whose relatives died in the war. That's why I changed my name back. In the documents, they listed my year of birth as 1938 so I became one year younger.

So I went to the dietsky dom in Kalininskaya but the Germans came there, too. All of us children stood in line and the Germans looked at us.

I don't know what happened but after this meeting with the Germans, every child had a problem with their eyes. Their faces were red and their eyes didn't open. Something bad had happened. So all these children were taken to the hospital in Kherson. They had several operations but nothing helped. Many children died. Only urinating helped. The doctors told us to wash our eyes with urine. That helped.

There is a monument in front of the school in Novopoltavka now, a soldier. The monument was made by Jews in memory of the Jewish people who died on the battlefield during the war.

After the war was over, my mother took me home and everything became normal.

I can't remember anything about my father. My father married my mother before going to the army. I was very small when he went away and died.

[She holds back tears]

New religions come here now, born-again Christians. One is called Fifties. They are Jehovah's Witnesses. They give us a lot of information. But we burn up their pamphlets. We don't go to their meetings.

ANATOLIA IVANOVICH, MARIA'S HUSBAND

I was born 16 September, 1937, in the city of Perogia and my grandfather lived in the next village called Zapodit.11

Before the beginning of the war, my father took me to my grandpa and grandpa told me that my father never cried. When my father took me here, he cried. He said something very bad was going to happen. Then the war began. And my father went to the war and nobody ever saw him again.

After the war was over, my mother and I decided to go back to Perogia to find something from our old home because we had nothing in Novopoltavka. We walked for two weeks and came to Perogia and saw that our house was ruined; destroyed absolutely. And we walked a week to get back home. That was my childhood.

My son, Sergei, my elder, he owns a cafe now in Kherson. The name of the cafe is Moinya. People ask, what does it mean? Moinya is short for Moise, my grandfather's name,

How did Maria and I meet? After I finished school here in the next village, seventh form, I became a tractor master. I worked in a motor-tractor group. The whole village was not very big. We used to work there. We were young and very friendly. The boys in the village were afraid of us because we were Jews and big and cheerful. Us boys came here for dances. But the local boys stayed away.

Maria and I fell in love and married. She gave me two sons, one of them, as I said, lives in Kherson, and the second lives in the next house to us here. He has two children, a boy and a girl.

Both of our fathers died in the war. Maria's father's name was Moise Rafkin. There was one thing that connected us: She had nobody and I had no father.

Maria's father died but not in the Great War. He was murdered in the war with Finland. It was in 1939 when Hitler and Stalin had a pact. Hitler wanted to see how strong the Russians were. That's why he provoked the war with Russia. As a result, 40,000 Finns were killed along with 400,000 Russian soldiers, one of whom was Maria's father.

During the war, the head of our kolkhoz was a real leader. Everything was very, very good under him. He helped everybody. When a young man went off to war, he would throw him a farewell party. The same for funerals. Every three months there was a meeting of all the kolkhoz people. The leader would make a speech pointing out what everyone had done as a way to congratulate them. We had an account in the bank. Everybody decided together what to do with the money. Insurance against a bad crop? Buy equipment? We got it all. It was a very fair system. But when that leader died, the new one came from the city with a university degree. He managed the kolkhoz for five years. He was not very good.

The government made us close down the kolkhoz in 1997. Now there are no jobs here.

Everyone has their cows and we sell milk to the government. This is the only way for us to live. A liter of milk in the city costs seven hryvnia. We sell it for 1.38. It is not easy to live this way.

Let me tell you about the Motor Tractor Stations, "MTS," we called them. They were part of the kolkhoz. Only in an MTS was there a tractor. But there were groups of tractor technicians in every village, "tractorists," who repaired and maintained the tractors.

In the '50s, all technical equipment was given to the kolkhoz by the MTSs. Then each kolkhoz had its own tractors. But now there are no more MTSs.

I tried to take one agronomy course from Agronifka.[10] I was a very good agronomist but the people there, they lied about me. They said that I made several animals die, that it was my fault. So I returned here. And I am now the father of the young man living in Kherson who is now a businessman.

Anatolia and Maria went on to discuss current economic issues. Anatolia did most of the talking. He compared prevailing prices for meat with those for vegetables. Vegetables are apparently now much more expensive. During Soviet times, his pension could buy seven tons of oil. Now Anatolia can buy only one ton.[11] Everyone now is

10. Presumably an educational organization.   RB

11. I do not know what sort of oil Anatolia was referring to here. - RB

receiving no more than the minimal pension and that, he said, is unfair because, for example, he and Maria have worked for 35 years each and they are receiving the same pension as people who have never worked at all.

[Maria appeared to be close to tears.]

BELA YAKOVLEVNA

I was born in 1936 in the village of Novopoltavka, a lovely place where terrible things happened. I had two sisters and two brothers, one brother was younger than me and the others were older. When this town was a kolkhoz, it provided a very good life for the five of us. We had a very old, very small gramophone on which we listened to records. The community was very rich then. We had all sorts of machinery.

Then the war started.

In 1941, My older sister was in Nikolaev working at the railroad station and learned that the Jewish people were in danger. She came to Novopoltavka all wounded and bloody because the Germans had bombed the railway station. She understood that it was time to evacuate. She said to our family, "We must leave immediately!" We took our clothes, our documents, and one cow and evacuated to the east.

We brought the cow with us because my younger brother was only one year old and my parents had to feed him. So we went to Beryozovskoye where we intended to get on a train.

But the town was empty. We entered some buildings and wandered through rooms that were also empty. My grandma and grandpa decided to go back to Novopoltavka along with one of my aunts who was pregnant at the time. She was about to give birth and felt sick. We decided that my grandparents were very old and wouldn't be killed. And it was impossible for my aunt to continue on. So the three of them returned. The rest of the family continued on to the East. They went by train. But two grandmothers, one grandfather, two aunts, and three small children went back to Novopoltavka. They arrived there in September, 1941, and they were killed.

My grandfather, my father's father, was, I remember, very religious. My maternal grandmother was not so devout. In fact, she didn't believe in God at all. She didn't go to synagogue; she just didn't believe in God. Neither do I. But I like all the traditions of the Jewish faith, all the holidays.

We had no contact with those family members who returned to Nikolaev. We did not get back there until 1946. It was only then that we were told the story of the tragedy. No Jews remained. None.

Only four families returned to Novopoltavka. Some remained in Russia, some settled in Nikolaev but only four families returned here.

We learned so much on the kolkhoz. I learned about sowing and harvesting. My father was a good farmer. He was taught by his father who was taught by the German settlers and by Joint.

The war was a time of great fear. My mother and my father were extremely upset. The only thing that helped them survive psychologically was that my sisters and I came back alive.

My older sister was a driver. She was taken into the army but was disappointed to discover that girls were not permitted to be drivers of tractors. All those women who were taught in Moscow to be drivers became drivers only of military cars, not tractors.

One of my sisters was a driver at the airport. Her name was Maria. She was the younger one. The older one was Tsela. She was a *zinichitka*. The amazing thing was that they remained alive and came home after the war. Tsela became an officer.

Once, when the rest of the family lived in evacuation, Tsela arrived for a visit. We saw her in uniform. She was so beautiful.

It was a very frightening time for a child. I was afraid of lighted windows in the evening. Shadows. Everything. It was paranoia. During our evacuation, we saw planes and everyone was ordered to darken all of the windows. And when I was a little girl, I used to go out of the house in the evening and would check to make sure that the windows were covered so that they would not be noticed by the German pilots. My brother and I hid under the table when there was an air raid.

I don't have memories of moving to the kolkhoz. I was too young. The Soviet Union in those days pushed people into collective farms but there were many who didn't want to join; many Jews didn't like the Soviet Union at all. Many moved to Argentina. Others with big families had no choice; they had no way to make a living, so they joined the kolkhoz.

Before the kolkhozy, there were private farms but soon cows, machines and so on were taken from individual farms and became the property of all—of the entire collective farm.

But there were successes, too. Our kolkhoz developed many wonderful vineyards and gardens.

My parents were among those who were pleased with the Soviet Union as well as with the kolkhoz. My father was the chief of the field team. My mother was a deputy of the village Soviet. We became rich—at least we were rich in the kolkhoz context. My father would go to Nikolaev often and he bought back toys, dresses, shoes for us; all kinds of things.

I was very young. I lived at home and had a good life. I had friends, girls, boys, clubs, dances; a very interesting life. I didn't go to kindergarten. My sisters' friends would come to visit and we all sang songs together. We went to the club. There were lectures, concerts, and plays. We had a really great life.

Everybody has very pleasant memories of those days. There were no empty farms. They were all flourishing. We had pigs, cows, chickens ... Everything.

But if only we had guns, my whole family would have fought the Nazis.

Then came the tragedy of September, 1941. The Germans had a list of all the Jewish people in Novopoltavka. They gathered them in one place and marched them through a street. One man wanted to save a Jewish baby. He thought the German soldiers wouldn't notice. He was caught and the Nazi soldiers shot him.

I could be anywhere now. I love Israel because so many of my relatives are there. But I want to live right here. After I married, we went to Kazakhstan on a job. We stayed for only a half year and then I asked my husband to let us return to this area, to Nikolaev. I missed my friends and family.

I had a good life growing up in Novopoltavka and Nikolaev is now my home. My parents never wanted to live in Israel either. This is the place we have always loved. Many of my friends who have been in Israel for a long time are still nostalgic for Nikolaev.

NATAL'YA ALEKSANDROVNA, TEACHER

A boy from the 8th form of our school, who is not a Jew, recently completed a class project, "The History of Our Village in Ukraine: The Jewish Colony of Novopoltavka," It is the work of only one student, you understand, not a subject that is taught in the schools.

This kid is very interested in history. He is an orphan and was brought up by his aunt. At the moment he is in Nikolaev attending university.

There were once over 1,000 Jews in this town and just a handful of others. Nine hundred Jews were murdered here during the Nazi occupation. Before that Nestor Machno, the anarchist guerrilla, killed 120 Jews here in a pogrom.

There are three mass burial sites here no more than fifty yards from each other. Two are for the Jews murdered by the Nazis—one for men and the other for woman. And the third is for the Machno victims. There are very few Jews left in this town, only two or three.

A room in our primary-secondary school building is devoted to the history of our village. It is a little museum. In it we have collected materials and artifacts about past citizens. It is not entirely about the Jews but they are prominently mentioned.

The plan is eventually to have one entire wall devoted to the war and another for the Jewish agricultural colony that once existed here.

We teach our children that it was not just Jewish people who suffered, it was also Ukrainians, Russians, Poles, Tatars. It was people, many people, who suffered. Each of our classes has the task of maintaining a particular monument honoring those who were killed by the Germans, not the fact that they were Jews or belonged to any other group.

When I myself was in school, we studied the war and the Jewish people who were murdered. The museum in our school is important. It is a big, important thing to me. I respect the memories of our soldiers, the victims, and everyone, Jewish people as well; all of our people. This is our history. That is what I try to communicate to the children.

We also know that it is not only Germans who are capable of

dreadful acts. We Ukrainians have plenty of our own skinheads today.

JOURNAL

As we stood chatting between the men's and the women's burial sites, three fourteen-year-old girls who were carrying bouquets of flowers approached the women's site. They deposited the flowers respectfully at the base of the small, identifying monument. One of the girls wore a Russian Orthodox cross. I asked if any of them were Jewish. None were. "We do this to remember, 'na pamyatz.'" they explained.

Bela Yakovlevna, although born here, does not visit often. I am not clear about her reasons. Today may be the first time that she has come here at all. This must be a very painful experience for her. But she is deeply involved. She has helped to raise money to erect the monuments. People from many countries send money to her.

The Novopotavka school resembles its American suburban equivalent, large, single-storied and functional. Its earlier incarnation was far more traditional and of course almost entirely Jewish as was everything else here. Bela's sister attended through eighth form. Then she attended the Ukrainian school in Novopoltavka. After graduating, she went into the army.

We chatted informally about education. Bela Yakovlevna said, "In our country people only want the diploma, not an education."

They don't have an internet connection in this school. But some of the children have one at home. Novoi Boog, a neighboring town, has a school that is now on line. "It is richer than this village," Natal'ya Aleksandrovna said.

"Our government gives 10,000 hryvnia—$1,250—each year to Ukrainian schools," she continued. "The Novoi Boog school chose to use the money to set up the internet connection. Novopoltavka used it for the museum. As a result we were able to raise sufficient funds for the museum but only for a year."

In response to my question, Natal'ya Aleksandrovna explained that the Novopoltavka school does nothing currently to address global warming or alternative energy. Natal'ya Aleksandrovna herself is quite interested in alternative energy but without the internet it is hard to learn much about it, she said, adding, "There are two types of people, those who use alternative energy and those who don't."

Bela Yakevlevna said, "I have a niece whose home is powered entirely by solar electricity."

Olga Ivanovna (Ukrainian, Russian Orthodox), translator, asked: "Why was Novopoltavka called 'a Jewish colony?'"

Bela Yakovlevna: "It began at the time of Catherine the Great. She sent Jewish people here and others as well. In the eighteenth century it was a vacant, unpopulated area. So Catherine decided to get people to settle here. It wasn't that she was so kind-hearted. She wasn't. I don't actually know why she did it. Later, Tsar Aleksandr I also sent Jews to colonize this area. Jews arrived from Latvia, Estonia, and Lithuania. They were forced to come. It was a very hard life for the settlers because they didn't know anything about farming. A lot of them died of hunger.

"Before the Revolution, Tsar Nikolai II asked Germans to come here and teach the Jews how to farm. Soon there was one street just of Germans and several streets full only of Jews.

"Jews are very clever. They are excellent students. They soon became excellent farmers, even better than the ethnic Germans. They began to build schools, hospitals, mills; doctors and dentists came. After the Revolution, Agro-Joint came to help. The Joint still helps. They bring medicine and other supplies. More settlers arrived in the 1920s and 1930s. They were not forced. They wanted to become farmers. That is how kolkhozy were created."

Natal'ya: "A lot of American evangelists, came here for a while toward the end of the Soviet era; then they moved back to America. This monument was organized by a pastor, a certain David Wilkerson who was one of the evangelists."

POWs

MIKHAIL GREGORIEVICH

In 1943, I went into the army. But first I worked at Makhachkala as a porter and after that I became a soldier.

In 1943, I was on the Russian front. Early in 1944, my arm was injured. I was taken prisoner by the Germans in March and put in a prisoner of war camp in Brest. I was there for a year and one month. The American soldiers came to Koningsberg and liberated us.

Russian military men arrived at our camp. A lieutenant said politely, "There is a bridge over there. You are free to walk across it. You may go home." So we walked. But when we arrived at New Brandenberg, I saw a bunch of other Soviet soldiers marching under a guard who was taking them back to Belarus. We were forced to join them.

In Belarus we stopped and the commander made us give him our guns and documents. He said that he would give us new ones. But that wasn't true. We were put in a train the next day that would bring us to Kemerovo in Siberia. We were told that we had to construct a new city there, to "build Communism" because we were guilty of something even though we were not charged with anything. We had been prisoners Germany. That was enough. I was sent to Siberia without a trial or even any charges. It was not until 1955 that I finally was allowed to come back to Nikolaev.

I got married in Siberia and had three children there. Now I have not only those three children but six grandchildren and six great grandchildren. And we live in Nikolaev. Things worked out well in the end.

BORIS GREGORIEVICH

My wife was evacuated to Uzbekistan and she remained there until after the war. I was captured by the Germans. After the Soviet Union invaded Germany, I was moved to a more distant prisoner of war camp where I remained for ten years.

A Slave Laborer's Story

ASYA MOYESEVOVNA

I went to the market to see if I could find some food. That was the day that the Germans came to take the Jews away. For some reason I decided to tell the Germans that I was Jewish. So they took me to Germany. My son was a year and a half old. He was very weak because we didn't have enough food.

My husband had a brother. He was a clever fellow but had only three fingers so he was not taken into the army. He remained in Tagonrog. He created a beautiful false internal passport for me, what the Germans call an "Ausweiss." It said "Russian woman" on it, not "Jew."

"Nadezhda Antonovna Ofsyanikova" was my new identity. Henceforth I was Russian by virtue of this document. When I was taken by the Germans, it was as a Russian girl, my confession of Jewishness was forgotten.

We were put on a train, me, my baby, my brother's wife; all of us were brought to Poland where we were sold as slaves. A family in Germany bought me. This was in August, 1943.

My owner was a German factory director. His plant was near Mannheim. "Yuhim & Breidenbach"[12] was the company name. Breidenbach had died earlier so by then it was only Yuhim. I was taken to Yuhim's house where he, his wife, his daughter and his daughter's children lived.

I found myself cooking for about ten fellow slave laborers who were working in this factory.

Surprisingly, these German people were very kind to me. They even gave presents to my child. And the family helped to feed my son. They were very generous. They gave us a lot of food. I had plenty of vegetables available from which I made borscht and shared it with other Russians who were working as slave laborers in Yuhim's factory.

This wonderful German family never told the police about my giving borscht to Russians. They understood and they let me help these people. When I first got there, they thought that Russian people are terrible but then they saw that my brother's wife and I bathed our babies and concluded that Russians cannot be so bad. Best of all, they helped me feed my son. He regained his health and started to walk at last.

I stayed there for two years. When I first arrived, I didn't dare speak German at all because with my Yiddish accent, they would know at once that I was Jewish. So at first I spoke only Russian. Then I started tentatively to speak German. They never acted as if they guessed my Jewishness. But my hostess, I noticed, was very

12. I transcribed those names phonetically. - RB

kind to Jewish people. Maybe she understood who I was but protected us anyway.

Then one day American soldiers came to Germany. They took us to Green Field Camp. And the war was over.

Later while I was still in Germany, I wrote three letters, one to my mom in Dobry, one to my aunt in Nikolaev, and another to an aunt who lived in Moscow. I asked the last one to send a telegram to my mother who was in Tashkent saying that my son and I were still alive. But she made a mistake and wrote not about "Asya" but "Vasya." My mother was very surprised to receive that letter.

My husband had also been taken into custody in Germany. At that time there was a practice that you could send a message by radio giving your location, your name, and who you are looking for. It was broadcast on German radio. Yuhim, my owner, heard it. He found my husband and took him to me.

Years later my sons tried to find that wonderful German family to thank them for all they had done for us but they were unable to find them.

Evacuation Tales

LYUDMILA ALEKSANDROVNA

We were evacuated—one of the last families—to the Caucasus. We were one of the last because my father couldn't bear to leave the station. The director of the station said to him, "You have two choices. Either 1) blow up the station or 2) give it to someone who will guard it." There is a lot of oil in this area. We did not want it to fall into the hands of the Germans.

An airport was near the MTS, the tractor station. The people there said that they would take care of it. So my father gave it to them in a written legal document. We were in the Caucasus, Turkmenia, when the Germans took Rostov-on-Don. So we moved again. We moved a lot. I saw many, many things then that I don't want to remember.

War is an awful time.

SOFIA IVANOVNA

When the war started in 1941, we were evacuated. The first time we came here was in 1929 and then in 1941we were resettled in different places, Caucasus, Kazakhstan, Georgia; many different places. In 1944, we returned to Crimea.

YFIM GREGORIEVICH

My brother finished the institute before the war. He became a radio technician, an engineer. Because of his profession he had to go to Siberia for work before the war. And I, along with the rest of my family, went to Siberia with him to save ourselves from the war. After the war, my brother brought television to Kherson for the first time. There was no station here. He built stations all over the Soviet Union.

My father had a brother who was a clock maker. He had two daughters. When it was time to evacuate during the war, he decided to remain right here. He was a friend of the rabbi at the synagogue. They were all killed.

ANNA ISRAELEVNA

We were living in Kalininskaya. On August 12, 1941, when the war reached us, my children and I needed to escape from the village. We crossed three rivers, the Don, the Dniepr, and the Volga. Where did we go? We evacuated to Kazakhstan.

When the Kherson oblast was freed from the Nazis in 1944, we returned to our home.

Evacuation took place in two phases. The first was when the war arrived and we left the village. We went to a small town near Stalingrad. The second phase was in June of 1942 when we were forced to leave Stalingrad. To do so, we had to cross the Volga. That was a problem. No local ferry was running—there were only private boats.

A lot of people tried to cross. In our group there were no men, just women, my mother, my five sisters and me. We also had five small children with us. The oldest was seven. A sailor took pity on us and said that because we had no men, he would take us across the river himself.

There were two boats in the river, both of them filled with oil. A bomb hit one and the burning oil flowed through the entire Volga which burst into flame. Somehow, miraculously, we did not get burned.

When we finally reached the eastern bank, we went straight to the railroad station and got on a train to Kazakhstan. It was much better for us there than in Kherson. We joined a kolkhoz right away because we were collective farmers. We knew agriculture and we knew kolkhozy.

We left Kalininskaya in October, 1941. We came first to a stanitsa, a small place near Stalingrad. We spent almost a year there. But we had to run away in June of 1942. Then we continued on to Kazakhstan. The ones who went by train got there faster. But there were very few trains from the stanitsa then. A lot of people wanted to go but there were only a very few places.

[She bursts into tears.]

Because we couldn't use the train, we went by river on a huge barge. There were many people; everyone was dirty, everybody had lice, no one could find enough to eat and children were crying from hunger.

When we finally got to this place in the Stalingrad oblast, we were given a flat to live in. We first took a bath. It was October and it was already cold. My sister and I went to the forest to find wood for heat but many of us children got sick. We were struck with what in Russian we call "chore"—you call it rubella. You needed to be in a warm place but it was winter then and we were freezing. My mother saved all those children because she found milk for them. She worked in a kolkhoz with cows so getting milk was not a problem for her.

We also needed a dark place and something red on the windows. So we kept the room dark. A neighbor, the wife of a soldier, also had a child who became sick. My mother asked the woman to give her this child because she was sure she could save him. But the woman refused her help. She was not interested because her husband was in the war and she was young and liked to party with men. So the child died.

LISA EFIMOVNA

Because my husband was an animal technician and because the

area was highly productive and dependent on animals, he was a very important man in the community. He once received an invitation to attend an animal exhibition. The military exempted him because his skills were needed at home. But he felt that he could not stand back while our country was invaded. He decided to fight.

He went to war in Zaporizhia City. For some time, I wrote to friends there to find out what happened to him. They didn't know. This was a time of terrible battles and if he was not in the list of the dead people, that was the best information we could get.

I went to the city of Nicholsk with my children. We were there for a while but soon we had to run because of the Germans. We had horses. When we got to Nicholsk, I gave the horses to the kolkhoz and I worked there. But when we had to leave, people said, "Take your horses and everything you have and run!" But our horses were stolen and we had to take a bull instead. I was afraid of the bull. I was only a tiny woman.

We soon decided to come back to Nikolsk because the Germans went on to someplace else. But after a short time the Germans returned and we again had to leave Nikolsk so we went to Elista. We were on a bus and, although everyone tried to use the main road, we took secondary roads near the water. The Germans destroyed the big roads. We survived only because our bus used small ones.

We had no money. We were to receive our payment on June 23rd but June 21st was the start of the war. Well, my father-in-law was a shoemaker and he had his tools with him. When we came to a village, he repaired shoes and people gave him food for his work.

Elista was in Kalmykia, an oblast far to the east on the Caspian Sea. When I was there, I received a postcard from a friend, an accountant's son. He was in Kazan and while there he received a letter from my husband that gave his address and unit. That's what he sent me on the postcard. I never saw my husband again but I write to him at that address even now almost 70 years later.

We had to leave Elista and decided to go to Uzbekistan further to the East. We arrived in Buxoro near Tashkent. The bulls, they were good. They were stronger than horses but they needed more food and water so we decided to go to Uzbekistan by train leaving the bulls behind. We left them with people who promised that they would not kill them.

We finally got to Uzbekistan. We were in some train station. We decided to find a kolkhoz somewhere to get work, maybe picking cotton. Anything. But my mother-in-law became sick, very sick with dysentery. She was taken to hospital while I stayed with my son and my father-in-law, his daughter, and her child. We went to a place where we could stay. I had no permission to visit my mother-in-law in the hospital but I would talk with her by shouting at her window. We had no money so I slept at the train station with the child. It was very uncomfortable. I had no money. But I had a pocket in my tallis and I exchanged it for two pieces of sugar so I had something sweet for my mother-in-law when she came from the hospital.

We had to leave again but we didn't know where to go. Wherever we went, we had to leave. We picked cotton but my son had an allergy to it and developed problems with his eyes. When my mother-in-law got sick at the station and went to sleep, somebody stole her false teeth. I announced, "I will give 200 rubles if the teeth are returned." They never were.

The kolkhoz was very bad. There was no choice. We were forced to stay there. Half of the family was with us. When we reached the place, I didn't like it. The conditions were terrible. I decided to go farther. But we were not allowed to leave. So, we decided to cheat the system. I told my sister-in-law to go to work and then to escape by train.

So we started to head to Buxoro in Uzbekistan where we lived for a long time during the war.

As I said, my father-in-law was a shoemaker so he was able to help us get a little food. He would sit on the streets with his tools. He would fix people's shoes and they would give him a bit of bread and things.

One Uzbek guy from the financial sector came and said that he would pay my father-in-law ten rubles a day. That man was awful. For ten days the man beat my father-in-law and told him that he would die under the street. It was terrible and frightening. I wrote to the military ministry describing the whole situation. I explained that we had no money and that my husband was fighting the war as a volunteer and that we are living under the worst conditions. And I reported that the man from the financial sector was trying to extort money from us. Inspectors came to the house to see what was going on. Several days later a man from the financial district came and promised that we would not be harassed again.

ASYA MOYESEVOVNA

My aunt, my grandmother, my grandfather and my other aunt were evacuated to Astrakan. My grandfather had a hard time of it because he refused to eat food that was not kosher, "trayf." He died as a result. But my grandmother didn't want to die so she ate everything. And she survived.

MIKHAIL GREGORIEVICH

Some rich Jewish men came to the villages and told everyone to remain there. Those who did were killed.

BORIS GREGORIEVICH

The rich Jews who came to tell us not to evacuate were not from Ukraine. They were maybe from Russia. They said, "Don't go." It is not clear to me even now what their motivation was.

I was evacuated in 1942. We traveled by train. When it stopped, people came to the train and gave us food to eat. People were very kind to the Jews.

ANNA IOSIFOVNA (RUSSIAN)/HANNAH SHIFREH (YIDDISH)

I am from a very poor family. We were evacuated and this helped us to survive. We went to Kerch and brought the cattle with us. We walked the whole way. For one month we walked. We milked the cows along the way and let the milk spill on the ground because we had no pails.

From Kerch we went by barge to the Caucasus. We gave our cattle to the place were the cattle were kept. Then we were brought to the wagons and the wagons brought us to Masdoc in the northern Caucasus on the River Terik.

We were there for one year but the Germans came so we were evacuated again, this time to Baku. I don't remember exactly where. We wanted to get tickets to get to middle Asia but we had no money.

We went as far as the Iran border. Then we found work there.

We worked hard and we came down with malaria and suffered from famine and cold. For salary, we were given five hundred grams of bread. My mother didn't work because she got sick. When the bread was distributed, we gave the first piece to my mother.

It was impossible to live there. So I took my two brothers and my mother and we hiked 200 kilometers into the mountains from the Iranian border to Nagordno-Karabach and then to relatives and acquaintances who lived there. It took us a month by foot. I had long braids and I washed them in the river. My father and sister stayed at the border to find work.

My mother, my two brothers, and I remained there for one month. And then we were reunited with my father and sister. That was in 1942 or 1943.

We had no money and so we begged for alms. I was not shy. Begging was our only hope. People gave us bread, not money. The Armenians treated us well. We dug pits and baked scones in them. They were very tasty. I remember the beautiful gardens there, Mulberry and nut trees. People gave us food and the mulberry tree berries were big. So we worked and survived.

As I finished 10th form, I was asked to go to the district office. I went 30 kilometers by foot. The district office asked me to work as a teacher in the schools. I took the job and taught Russian to the children.

My Russian was not that great. I had only a 3—a "C"—in Russian. But I taught Armenians who knew less Russian than I did. So I translated for the Armenian teachers and they translated for me.

There was another teacher. But she didn't know Armenian—only Russian and that not so well.

I taught boys. The military committee told me to teach boys who didn't go into the army. I taught them Russian words.

In 1943 and 1944 the Russians liberated Crimea. In 1944, we returned to our homes. We told everybody that the Armenians had saved us and helped us to survive.

My brother, the one who was in the army, was rewarded by the order of the Red Banner. I wrote him a letter. I asked him to help me help our family survive. The letter traveled slowly. My family and I were in Armenia when my brother received the letter. He sent his answer to Baku and asked if anyone knew where we were. His letter went first to Baku, then to Armenia and finally to the kolkhoz in Armenia. The result was that he did help our family survive.

Eventually we got to be rich because the kolkhoz helped us.

IRINA ALEKSEEVNA

My grandparents on my father's side decided not to be evacuated to the East and so they were killed here.

OLGA SIMONOVNA

In 1936, my brother and I went to school. My brother was one year older than me and took part in the war. He died in 1956. During the war he was lost for two years. We didn't know anything about him. But finally he was found.

The war came to us on September 28, 1941. When the German soldiers were almost in Crimea, we took all the domestic animals to Kuban through the sea route. We lived in Kuban until the Germans came to Rostov-on-Don for the second time. Then we had to escape. But we could take only the most important things with us because there was no time.

For seventeen days, we walked. It was slow and difficult. Fortunately, we were able to get to Baku and from there to Krasnozavodsk. Then all of us evacuated people were sent to different places by the officials. My family was sent to Pavlodarskaya oblast to one of the kolkhozy that was very far away. They had no school there.

We then started to look for my mom's sisters. There was a city called, "Buguruslan" and people could find their relatives through that city because that was where lists of people were kept. We found my mom's younger sister but only her. She lived in Kazakhstan in the eastern region, Ust-Kamenogorsk.

We were very poor by that time so we wrote a letter to my mom's sister asking for help. She sent us 300 rubles.

We were so very poor, so poor that we didn't have any food. So my dad went to other kolkhozy to earn a little money. He didn't find work for a long time. Someone finally gave him something to eat. But because he hadn't eaten for so long, he got sick. We were waiting for my dad to return but he didn't. My brother went to look for him saying, "I will find him dead or alive!" And he found him alive and brought him home, very sick, nearly dead and all that my dad had earned was a little bag of leftovers.

Back then when we were running away to the "Prevail," the area connecting Crimea with Ukraine, there was only one path, a very narrow one with a mountain on one side and a steep cliff on the other. There were thousands of people running away along the same narrow path. Since we were escaping in the dark, a lot of horses fell down the cliff. Many children also fell.

This is what I remember. But we were not afraid. We were only thinking of how to escape.

As we were running away on the cart pulled by horses, we needed to cross the river on the bridge but there were so many people and domestic animals who were trying to cross at the same time that we lost some of our kolkhoz people. My dad went to see where they were and found them at the head of the line as we were waiting way back for our turn to cross the bridge. The people in the kolkhoz respected my father a lot. He was a good leader. A lady from our kolkhoz saw my father and said that my dad could take his family and join her group, skipping to the head of the line. He thanked her.

Then he came back to us and took us through the line, explaining to people that he and our family were part of the kolkhoz contingent crossing the bridge already and that we needed to cross with the rest of our kolkhoz members. So we joined the others. And we crossed

Immediately afterwards, the bridge collapsed.

I Still Hear Her Voice

OLGA SIMONOVNA

We ran away from the Germans but we barely escaped. Once we were surrounded by them. I don't know how we got away. We could not take many of our belongings with us. The only things I rescued were portraits of Lenin and Stalin and two red Pioneerskaya kerchiefs because they was so dear to me.

When we were surrounded by the Germans, three Kuban Cossacks suddenly appeared to help us escape. I told my mother afterwards, "Mom, I am going to bury these portraits and the kerchiefs right here and I will dig them out again when we come back to this place." But we never did return.

We found ourselves in a village when the Germans almost got there. We needed to get away fast so we went to the train station. The station was overflowing with people including families that also wanted to escape but there were no trains for civilians. All the trains were reserved for the army. So we waited.

All of a sudden, a man entered the station and asked, "Is there anyone here who can milk a cow?" My mom answered, "I can milk a cow. What will you give me for doing that?" The man said, "What do you want?" My mom said, "A cart and horses for my family."

The man said, "Okay. I will give you a horse and a cart."

So the man, my family, and another family who asked if we would take them with us, got into the cart and went to get the cows to milk. But when we came to the place the man wanted to take us to, there were no cows. We couldn't find the cows anywhere.

The Germans were very close so we decided to run further without the cows. We ran until dark. Then we saw a haystack and decided to spend the night there because we had that other family with us that included a five-year-old child and a blind old lady.

Since it was dangerous to travel during the day, we walked at night only. We were always hungry. Whenever we saw Russian soldiers, my mom would go up to them to ask for food, saying, "I have kids. I don't have anything to give you. Do you have anything to give us?" And our wonderful Soviet soldiers, they always shared everything with us.

My mom was only 40 years old but by then she looked like a very old lady. She was always looking for food for us, roots or vegetables, anything she could find to feed us kids.

When we were running for 17 days, we met three army deserters from the Red Army. We walked along with them. They were in front of us walking faster. We would lose each other for a while and then we would meet again. The last time I met them, I said, "Can't we please wait for our parents because I am afraid my parents may be lost? They don't know which way to go."

We came to the crossroad. There was a way to the left, another to the right and a third straight ahead. The soldiers said, "If you go to the left, you will run into the Germans. You must go to the right."

I begged, "Please, please wait for my parents. Don't go on without us. I will give you everything I have." I had a little bit of food and 20 rubles in a box with me.

So the soldiers said, "Come with us to the right. We will show you how to escape. Then you will come back and take your parents with you."

So we did and then I came back for my parents. I ran along the road screaming for them by name. They could hear me but I couldn't hear them until we finally met. We met at the crossroad.

My dad kept insisting that we needed to go left which was where the soldiers had said that the Germans were encamped. My dad was sure that left was the correct route because he saw the footprints of the horses on the ground but I tried my best to convince him not to go that way but to the right instead. I kept saying and saying this, shouting louder and louder. Finally I convinced him and my mother to go to the right, the correct way according to those guys.

So we went to the right. And we were okay.

Then the blind old lady asked for water. For some reason her grownup children didn't do anything at all for her. So my brother found a cup or something to bring her water from the river.

Her kids kept right on sitting there doing nothing. The next morning, everybody began climbing up a steep hill to get out of there and continue our escape. Someone gave me a stick for climbing.

Just then we realized that our mother was not with us. Where was our mom? So we started screaming, "Mom! Mom! Where are you?"

I looked back and there I saw my mom with the blind old lady and I realized that the blind, old lady's kids were already up on top of the hill. They had left her where she was. And my mom stayed with her to help.

But my mom couldn't do anything because the blind old lady could hardly walk. So my mom had to climb the steep hill alone to join us. When we all got to the top of the hill, we were shocked to see that the woman's children and grandchildren had left her down at the bottom alone.

My mom begged to return for that babushka but my dad wouldn't let her because it would have been impossible to climb the hill again especially with the blind old grandma.

There was no way to bring her up and we were so upset that her children never tried to do anything to help us rescue her!

I still remember how that old, blind *babushka* cried and screamed, and called each one of her children by name. She screamed and cried every single person's name. I still remember that scream and that cry.

I worry that she may have eventually been eaten by wolves.

For years her voice remained in my ears.

When we got to the city, my dad was afraid that there was no wood to burn for heating.

September, 1945 was when we moved back to the kolkhoz. The war was over. I was 17 years old. I said, "Mom and dad, you stay here. I will move to the city and live with my aunt Vera."

But my parents decided to move with me. We went to synagogue and met some people. These people helped us find a little nine-meter room for our family.

Once I returned to the kolkhoz to visit that family we had escaped with. The husband had just got back from a POW camp in Germany and brought some stuff with him. A lot of stuff. They never gave me anything. I didn't care. I just remember that there was a portrait of that blind old babushka on the wall and I said to the lady, "That is your grandma."

She said, "Oh, you remember her?"

"I still hear her voice in my ears," I answered.

Old Friends

BORIS GREGORIEVICH

I was born in1924 but my passport reads 1923 because I lied about my age so I could to join the army. The two of us grew up in Dobry. We went to school there and studied the German, Russian, and Ukrainian languages. Yiddish, too. We learned German because there were a lot of German people who worked with us in the factory.

MIKHAIL GREGORIEVICH

I am much younger than him. I was born in 1925. I remember a lot from my childhood. When we were very young, all we did was play and ride horses and avoid helping our parents.

Boris: In Dobry, all the men worked hard but the women didn't. They took care of their children. Families were very big in those days. Often there were a half dozen children in a family. People didn't get salaries for their work. But they did get vegetables, wheat, and so on. When children went to school, the kolkhoz gave them food. There were about a thousand or maybe fifteen hundred people in Dobry in those days.

Mikhail: Dobry was very large. It was divided into two parts and separating the two was a river. In the last days of the year, we received wheat from the kolkhoz, about two or three kilograms for each day that we worked. During the year that was ending we earned credit for working days. Through the year, a person could collect maybe up to five hundred days. We sometimes got as much as two to three credits for each day we worked.

Where did we store all that produce? We didn't; we used it right away. We made bread, seven or eight loaves that would last the whole week. There were very big stoves in each house where we would bake. You can't find such delicious bread now. There are no stoves anymore like ours.

Boris: There were three small villages right together. People married each other, not from the city but only from the adjoining villages where there were Jewish people.

Mikhail: There were three children in my family. My father worked.

Boris: In my family there were also three children. My father was a machinist but he worked as a porter because there were no machines. We did everything by ourselves. Everyone was very honest. Nobody stole.

Mikhail: My father worked in the kolkhoz but my mother did not. Only my father's work counted as a registered workday. My mother was just a housewife. She took care of the children. My parents had several pieces of land. One of them was their own plot for growing their own vegetables.

In Dobry at the time there was a birthing house. It was like a hospital for obstetrics.

Boris: I fought the German soldiers and then, after the 9th of May, 1945, Victory Day, we were taken to fight the Japanese. That's why I am so ill to this day. I was injured.

Mikhail: My daughter, she is now in Israel. She asks me to write my autobiography. But we hesitate to tell our stories because we don't think that anybody needs that information. It is all in the past. Nobody wants it. Nobody is interested.

Boris: In my whole life you want to know what stands out? I think that in the old days people were friendlier and kinder to each other than they are today. We celebrated birthdays and holidays together. That was back in the time of the settlements. Nobody was killed then. People were close. Now everyone is scattered.

I was awarded many medals. I even got one from Israel to celebrate 50 years of victory.

Mikhail: I read in the newspapers about Lvov. Some people asked our president not to make the 9th of May such a big victory day. That was not a good suggestion. May 9th is a great holiday celebrating our victory. In Lvov there were people who were aligned with the German soldiers. It is only for them, that it was not such a big thing.

So what stands out the most for me? I remember I had a boat and I went fishing and then I sold my boat and now I don't have anything.

So now? The expense of medicines is terrible and food prices are high. But the khesed gave us clothes. That helps.

Oh, but we still have good times. People came here from America to sing Yiddish songs. Boris sings very well. He sang for them and they paid him for it. That was a wonderful evening.

[Boris breaks into a sad Yiddish song. Mikhail joins in.]

V
What Next?

ALEKSANDR ZAKHAROVICH

After the war, I got a job at the Institute of Agriculture. From the 15th of November, 1947, until the 12th of May, 2010, I worked there. Sixty-two years. I loved my career. I retired only because my wife was getting ill and needed care.

My work brought me much satisfaction and many honors. Even now I continue to work on many projects. I have always been an agronomist. Agriculture has been my life. It still is.

Maya, my wife, has spent 40 years in journalism. She was editor-in-chief of Crimean television. She retired at age 60.

LYUDMILA ALEKSANDROVNA

After the war my family stayed in the 62nd District where they were before the war. I moved to Simferopol to get an education and from that time on, I have lived here. Then my whole family moved to Simferopol.

This was 1948 or so. The kolkhozy kept on going but they were making things in other ways, not just off the land.

Some kolkhozy survived until 1991 or so. Maybe even later. But after perestroika, they deteriorated. They got really bad. Many settlements are now destroyed; they no longer exist. There is nothing left. I haven't visited any f them but that's what I was told.

ANNA ISRAELEVNA

After the war in 1949, we constructed a monument. We wrote letters to the entire Soviet Union to find citizens of this village who survived in Kazakhstan or on the battlefields. We wanted to know who was still alive. Since then, on every September 16th or a little later, we visit this monument. I try to visit every year and will do that for as long as I can. I taught my children to visit this monument, too, and they teach their children to visit it in memory of the people who were killed for nothing, only because they were Jews.

LISA EFIMOVNA

In 1944, the 13th of March, we learned that the Kherson region had been liberated. We made food for the road home and by December, we returned to Kalininskaya. But when we get got there, we discovered that our house was not empty. A Russian woman was living there who had been the head of our kindergarten. She said, "Of course, I will give you your home back," but she only gave us one room. And she hid all our things that we left at home.

My father-in-law died but not because of the action of a young financial inspector who falsely accused him of corruption. He was simply very old.

When I got back to Kalininskaya, we set up a dietsky dom in Kaliningrad. Another woman and I gathered orphans who were living in abandoned buildings and I taught there until 1972 when I retired.

In 1989, I moved to Kherson.

During the war 600 people died in our village. That was out of a total of over 1,000. After the war, the survivors gathered monthly at a monument they built for those people.

LYUDMILA ALEKSANDROVNA

After the war there were many reminders of the war including scraps of metal on the fields. Children climbed and played on the destroyed weapons at the aerodrome.

The smallest of the boys let me play with them. The boys threw bullets into the flames of bonfires they lit. Some of them got injured. I did not.

IRINA ALEKSEEVNA

My paternal grandmother had a house in Kherson where we all lived. She was killed by the Nazis. During the war a family headed by a Soviet officer came and appropriated our house. When our family returned, we were allowed at first to occupy only a few rooms. Then we were forced to move out entirely. My father refused to move. He said, "This land came from the blood of my parents." But they forced him out.

That grandmother said to my grandfather, "If he"—my father—"stays, a tractor will come and destroy the house with him in it."

What a tragedy.

Retirement

INA YAKOVLEVNA

I have been a teacher for many years. Just recently students I had 40 years ago gave me a party in appreciation. I was very touched.

I will be 80 on the first of August. I have one younger sister who lives in Israel. She is younger by 15 years so we did never had a close relationship.

I have worked at two different schools during my career. The first was School Number Nine in Nikolaev where I spent 15 years. I worked with all the secondary school classes from sixth form to eleventh form, young people 12 through 17 years of age. My specialty was physics. Then I became an inspector of the schools. But I continued to teach physics and astronomy as well but not for a full day, only a half day. I retired at age 60.

I never had any problems with discipline because at the first lesson, I always said to the children, "Look at me: keep your eyes right on me and be silent. You must be able to hear your own heart."

I could have worked beyond age 60 but my husband was ill and I needed to retire in order to take care of him. I stayed at home with him until 1994 when he died.

Now I live alone in my own apartment. It has three rooms. For our city, that is considered a big flat.

The difference in age of my sons is 13 years. Our elder son is a teacher; the younger one is a doctor.

My big problem now is economic, paying for the apartment. It used to cost me 17 rubles per month. Now we've switched to the Ukrainian hryvnia—which is worth the same as a ruble—and it costs 400 hryvnia. That is equivalent of 50 dollars. It doesn't sound like a lot to Americans but it is a huge sum for Ukrainian retirees. And this bargain price is for those people who were participants in the war. Other people pay even more.

My pension is 1,120 hryvnia. It is very little; almost impossible to live on. Fortunately, the khesed helps me buy medicine. If not for that, I would not survive. The Ukrainian government provides no help at all beyond its inadequate pension.

I was ten when the war started. I had finished only the first two forms then.

My father worked in the Nikolaev port. He was the chief accountant and was so good that the government exempted him from the army. We were evacuated to the North Caucasus to the city of Voroschilov now known as Grozny, the capital of Chechnya. We took only two suitcases with us because we thought we would be back in three months.

I was never put into a German prison camp because we ran away and hid. As a result, I am not receiving reparations from the Germans which would have come in handy now.

I read a lot. I like newspapers. Unfortunately I don't have enough money to buy everything I want. My sons help me as much as they can. I have an old computer that I like to use. I can get on line. I find that interesting.

I have some relatives in other countries. My grandmother, for example, had two brothers who emigrated to Buenos Aires many years ago but I don't know their surnames.

I go to the Jewish Community Center maybe three times a month. I have friends there. We talk; maybe we go to the theater together. I made four visits to the seashore with them last year.

We once went to a sanatorium in Chernomoriya. And we were observed there by doctors. Such a thing can happen only with the help of the khesed.

There are little clubs in our Jewish community. They appeared a very long time ago; they were called "warm houses." In my club there are twelve people. We celebrate birthdays together. It is very nice.

But it is only the Jewish Community Center that helps—along with the khesed. I don't know what happens to other people when they get old, the non-Jews, the Ukrainians, for example. A lot of old people suffer from loneliness and depression in this country. Relationships, things to do, and contacts of any kind are very important; absolutely essential.

My own hobby is writing. I write and my group always awaits new material from me.

It is very hard being old and dependent on pills, operations, and doctors. If I hadn't had a son who is a doctor, it would be impossible for me to be operated on and taken care of properly. It was only because of my son that I am surviving well.

It is still sometimes free to see the doctor as it was under the Soviets. But you must pay for medicines. I must take "Preductal." It had cost 62 hryvnia for a month's supply only a few years ago. Now it costs 120 which is impossibly expensive,

I live in a house where there are a lot of Russian retirees, not Jews. I have good relationships with them. We speak freely. But I don't tell them that I have help from khesed because they would feel bad.

Before the election, Yanukovich, our Prime Minister, promised, "I will listen to every person in this country." He also promised that if elected he would increase the pension by five times, five hundred percent. Five times. But he lied. The truth is that during this period my pension was increased by only fourteen hryvnia.

Our Prime Minister is an ass. I found an article by him in one newspaper with the title, "Unnecessary People." In it he wrote, "Our country cannot afford so many retirees."

There is a government program I forgot to mention. It is only for people who do not have children and who own an apartment. People are sent in to help them. That's fine. But when they die, the apartment goes to the government.

I live on the fifth floor in my building and there is no elevator. I must rest three times as I walk up the stairs. When my husband had a heart attack, our doctor said that it is very good that we live on the fifth floor because walking up those stairs was the only exercise he could get in this city.

I have thought about going to Israel. But my sons are here—although I do have a grandson in Israel. Well, I belong here. This is where I feel most at home despite everything.

I think things were a lot better under the Communists. People here of my age don't care about Democracy or Communism or the independence of Ukraine. We only want enough to live on.

I don't THINK things were better under the Communists. I KNOW that they were.

So many problems. So many problems.

Today

ALEKSANDR ZAKHAROVICH

I am now 86. I was born on December 15, 1924. I was five at the time I have told you about. I was young then; now I am old but I remember a lot.

With perestroika, Gorbachev closed most of the remaining kolkhozy. The end of USSR in 1989 brought with an end to collective farms although a few remained in some places possibly even to this day. People often assume that they disappeared immediately after the war but nobody, neither journalists nor historians, have come here to research this question.

It is unfortunate, I believe, that kolkhozy no longer exist.

LYUDMILA ALEKSANDROVNA

I have been on pension since 1983. It used to be easy to live on a pension. But now it is very hard. Impossible. I was once able to go to Moscow to buy things every now and then but I can't do that anymore. Now everything is extremely difficult for me.

A person cannot live on 800 hryvnia—$100—in Ukraine. The khesed helps out. But it is still extremely hard.

When my husband died, we were living on the fourth floor and my house, the building where our apartment was located, was not properly maintained. It had deteriorated badly. It got so bad that my son sold the apartment and he, his family and I, found one on the ground floor. Now we all live there.

I don't know how much my son paid for the apartment. But life is hard for a lot of people now in Ukraine. It is very difficult. There are many people without work. My son is one of them. He lost his job.

That's how it is.

SOFIA IVANOVNA

I had a lot of friends. Even now there are six of us, all about 80 years old. We get together once a month, all six of us. Six birthdays every year and at other times we just sit and talk. We play all sorts of games like the old ladies that we are, card games mostly. All of our husbands have died. Only old ladies are left.

We were friends when we were young. We were friends when we met our husbands and we are still friends now that we have lost our husbands. I try to be active, not just sit at home and be bored. We go to the parks to see flowers. Even after I retired, I continued to work. It is only for the past two years that I have not worked any more. Besides work, I had always been active in the community life.

My husband died 16 years ago. He was my first and last love. We studied together at the technical school. There were not so many girls at the technical school then but a lot of guys. We got married right away. All of my friends also met their husbands at that school. My friends and I help each other all the time. If someone calls ask for help or anything, I do everything I can. The same if I need someone's help.

YFIM GREGORIEVICH

My brother died in 1994 in Israel. My sister is in Germany and is 91 years old. My other sister died in 1963. There were four of us.

ANNA ISRAELEVNA

An organization in California helps me. I sent them a newspaper article that explains what has happened to me. This organization is interested in me. They send me photographs and they gave a dinner in America to honor me.

LISA EFIMOVNA

I am now an old pensioner. I live on medications. I am very ill. I take so many medicines. I know that people in America have similar problems. My first husband died. I married again. But my second husband also died. Now my family consists of 29 people. A grand-child is pregnant so I am waiting for the thirtieth.

Everyone treats me with respect and has a place in my soul. My second husband left me with richness, two sons. My third son is from my first husband. All my sons help me. I live not such a bad life.

ANNA IOSIFOVNA (RUSSIAN)/HANNAH SHIFREH (YIDDISH)

I retired and was rewarded for having worked in a concrete factory. I received many honors. I worked there for 36 years, first as an engineer in labor and then as an economist-engineer.

MIKHAIL GREGORIEVICH

I don't want to live with my children. One is in Israel; two others live in Russian cities. I went twice to Israel but it is too hard for me there.

A Yiddish Lilt

APRIL 22, 2011, THE LAST DAY: JOURNAL

I awoke early this morning and walked about near the hotel. It was not a pretty scene. Two elderly women in blue smocks were sweeping up the massive trash carelessly strewn there from the previous ordinary day. They wielded handmade brooms consisting of twigs bunched and tied together. One fellow, not very old, in his thir-ties perhaps, sat crunched behind them in a wheelchair. His right leg was missing. He took an occasional swig from a bottle balanced precariously on his lap. His skin was blotched and red. His clothes had probably not been changed for a very long time. A perky young woman walked over to him and gave him an apparently gratuitous scolding, the meaning of which I could not grasp. I imagine that she instructed him to get his act together, to stop drinking....

This is the last day of my research project. I am now back at Khesed Shimon in Simferopol awaiting the arrival of the very last two interviewees. My latest translator, Sonya, an obviously intelli-gent high school student who has been studying English, has just arrived.

I have been set up at a desk in a small performance room. A stage with a piano on it is at the far end opposite me. Eleven senior citizens, ten women and one man, are practicing upbeat songs for what I imagine is going to be a performance. Snacks are arranged prettily on a table.

Khesed Shimon sponsors many activities for people who live in the area, older people and younger ones, too. That's nice for them but here I am, cooling my heels. No way can I interview anybody with all that singing going on. I've been here for fifteen minutes already. How much longer …?

Misha Goldenberg, the director of the Jewish Community Center in Nikolaev—the city where I was yesterday—and board member of Nikolaev's khesed, explained that a khesed is really just a social-service organization. It was for this reason he believed that in Nikolaev there was room for a community center as well. But here in Simferopol, the distinction between the two sorts of institutions does not seem to hold. Neither was it the case in Kherson. In both cities, the local khesed played the social-service and the community center roles simultaneously and with considerable vigor. Something cultural was going on in each of those kheseds beyond mere social service functions. Sometimes it involved old folks. Sometimes children.

No way we can do interviews in this room. Not quiet enough. Maybe Natasha, my friend the program director, set me up here for the sake of my own entertainment while I wait for interviewees to show up.

Aha! Natasha herself has just appeared and has joined the celebrating group. Everyone is now standing in a circle and has burst into a cheerful song directed at one of their members, a certain "Rita," who is being congratulated. Perhaps it is her birthday. Russians, including Russian Jews, are in the habit of using the international "Happy Birthday to You" tune, the same one we use. For all I know, the words are the same.

Now they are onto singing something else. It has a Yiddish lilt although the words are Russian. They hand her gifts, flowers mostly. She is all smiles.

Time to eat. They are crowded around the serving table munching snacks and appear quite social in a manner of a suburban American school, church, or synagogue. But I stay put, clear of the scene, because I am not part of the group and my Russian remains marginal.

It has improved somewhat on this visit, but still remains at the Chico Marx level.

The sense of community is strong: My God! These are my people, deeply so even though I cannot communicate with them very well. Their manners, their looks, their ways of walking and talking, all are fully, happily familiar.

It is good that I have my own work to do as I peer surreptitiously at them or it might be awkward. For their parts, they are well aware of my presence and that I am a foreigner yet they have some sense of what my project is all about and obviously support it. I am not therefore an intruder. I have a legitimate place here and a social role, too, based in history.

A smaller group, eight of the originals, are now back to rehearsing songs. Another woman, the leader, is at the piano, pounding on it, coaxing the group along and suggesting changes in how they perform the music. It occurs to me that the melodies are more in the Russian style than the Yiddish. The Yiddish language has been lost in this homeland. Lost, too, are many of the personal characteristics of residents of the pre-Hitler Jewish world. Yet something very Jewish remains.

What is it?

VI
Photographs

Further Readings

Deckel-Chen, Jonathan L. *Farming the Red Land: Jewish Agricultural Colonization and Local Soviet Power, 1924–1941.* Yale University Press, 2005.[13]

Hoffman, Charles E., *Red Shtetl: The Survival of a Jewish Town under Soviet Communism,* The American Jewish Joint Distribution Committee, 2002.

Mendelsohn, Ezra. *The Jews of East Central Europe between the World Wars.* Midland Books, 1987.

Morrissey, Evelyn. *Jewish Workers and Farmers in Crimea and Ukraine.* Privately printed, 1937.

Reid, Anna. *Borderland: A Journey through the History of Ukraine.* 1997, Westview Press.

Rosenberg, John. *On the Steppes.* Borzoi Books, 1927.[13]

Snyder, Timothy. *Bloodlands: Europe between Hitler and Stalin.* Basic Books, 2010.

Weinberg, Robert. *Stalin's Forgotten Zion: Birobidzhan and the Making of a Soviet Jewish Homeland.* University of California, 1998.

---

13. My father, Max Belenky, is interviewd in these books. He is the man on the far right on the cover of "Farming the Red Land."

Glossary

AGRO-JOINT, JOINT OR THE JOINT, non-governmental organization in the Soviet Union that supported Jewish land settlers. Affiliated with the American Jewish Joint Distribution Committee.

AMERICAN JJWISH JOINT DISTRIBUTION COMMITTEE, JDC, organization devoted to worldwide relief efforts.

BABUSHKA, kerchief; "grandmother."

BUND, The Jewish Bund was a secular Jewish labor party before the Revolution,

DIETSKY DOM, children's house; orphanage.

FOOTBALL, soccer

GREAT PATRIOTIC WAR; World War II

HECTARE, 2.47 acres.

HUTOR, section of a village.

KADET, "Constitutional Democratic Party," liberal and pre-Soviet.

KHESED, a Hebrew word that may be translated as, "Loving kindness." A community-based social service agency or center.

KOLKHOZ, Russian acronym for "collective farm." Kolkhozy, plural.

KOMSOMOL, Russian acronym for "Young Communist League."

KOMZET, Soviet organization for obtaining and distributing land to Jews.

KULAK, a peasant, allegedly affluent, often not, persecuted by the Soviets as an enemy of the state.

LISHENTSY, people disenfranchised by the 1918 constitution because of membership in the "exploiting classes."

LUFTMENSCHEN, from the German meaning "air people" to describe those, especially Jews, whose living is derived from words, trading or money-lending.

MESTETCHKA, Russian translation of "shtetl."

MTS, Machine Tractor Station.

NEW ECONOMIC POLICY; NEP, Lenin's experiment in limited capitalism.

OBLAST, large district around a city, "province."

OBSCHINA, community. Obschinach, plural.

OZET, "The Society for the Settlement for Jewish Toilers on the Land."

PALE OF SETTLEMENT, the area between western Russia and eastern Poland where Jews were permitted to live before the Revolution.

PASOLUK, farm community.

PIONEERSKAYA, a youth organization, the Young Pioneers.

RAYONNE, neighborhood, subsection of a district.

SHTETL, town inhabited by Jews.

STANITSA, term referring to a rural community especially in Southern Ukraine

STARIK, old man.

TALLIS, traditional Hebrew prayer shawl.

ZINICHITKA, Anti-aircraft gunner.

About the Author

I grew up in New York's Greenwich Village during the frothy 1930s and 1940s. My family, never far from its Russian roots, was, like that of most of my friends, artistically inclined, secular Jewish, and politically on the humanistic left. My father's work in the Soviet Jewish land settlement movement informs this book.

Before my birth, my mother was a preschool teacher trained in the Dewey tradition. I was therefore sent to remarkable progressive schools until college at Cornell. Next I received a Ph.D. in clinical psychology from Teachers College, Columbia University, once a hotbed of Deweyan pedagogy.

My work life has been with children in schools, communities and institutions. For fifteen years my office was in a Vermont forest where kids and parents would come for a day or so to think through personal or family issues.

On retirement in 1995, I began a series of visits to Haiti and Russia in order to learn how young people may be helped to grow up when natural families are unavailable. I have written several books and have taught at Harvard, Boston University, and Concordia University. I was the founding dean of Goddard College's individualized master's degree program. Recently, I embarked on a study of my family's history. The present book reflects that interest.

Mary Field Belenky, a developmental psychologist, and I have been married for over fifty years. We have two children, five grandchildren, and one dog.

CPSIA information can be obtained at www.ICGtesting.com
Printed in the USA
BVOW070349121012

302805BV00001B/8/P